THE YOUNG PRIEST

THE YOUNG PRIEST

GASTON COURTOIS

HERDER AND HERDER

1965
HERDER AND HERDER NEW YORK
232 Madison Avenue, New York 10016

Original edition: *Jeune Prêtre*
(Éditions Fleurus, Paris).
Translated by Michael C. O'Brien.

Nihil obstat: Brendan Lawlor
              Censor Deputatus

Imprimatur: Patrick C. Brennan
              Vicar General, Diocese of Burlington
              October 9, 1964

Library of Congress Catalog Card Number: 65:13488
© 1965 by Herder and Herder, Incorporated
Printed in the United States of America

Contents

1 THE PERSONAL LIFE OF THE YOUNG PRIEST

Though it may seem paradoxical at first sight, the most important point in the ordering of the young priest's life, the one that directs all the others, is to get to bed early enough to assure sufficient sleep.

The amount of time needed for a good night's sleep varies according to temperament, but according to present health standards, seven hours is the minimum, and eight hours is an honest mean.

Be on your guard: carried along by your zeal and overwhelmed with work, you may risk stealing from your time of sleep. Yet these demands on your time usually result less from the accumulation of responsibilities imposed by superiors than from an increase of occupations through inexperience and lack of organization.

Later, when you have attained the fullness of maturity, perhaps you can safely allow yourself a few prolonged night vigils. But, in your first years, be very prudent. Without your being aware of it, lack of rest will make you more excitable, more nervous, more susceptible. All your efforts at prayer or study will be more difficult and less fruitful.

Going to bed a half-hour early once in a while may

gain for you in both quantity and quality hours for the morning.

Do not object that you have evening meetings, rehearsals, etc. . . . Your young people too need sleep. It is ill service you render them by giving them the example of staying out late. Under normal circumstances, there should be no regular meeting that lasts beyond 10:00 P.M.

You left the seminary with the idea of doing as much good as possible. And you are right. But the greatest apparent good is sometimes the enemy of the real good. To do the greatest good is not to desire to do indiscriminately all the good that presents itself.

Consider the first years of your ministry a practical stage in reaching perfection, or more simply an apprenticeship. Be content not to do immediately all the good you see to be done. This is often hard, but it is not necessary to harvest before the grain is ripe. If you let yourself be crushed by tasks multiplied beyond your present abilities, you will compromise the good which you would be able to do later, in a few years, at the age of maturity and responsibilities.

This does not mean being overly careful, but it means not overworking yourself. Some most promising priests have not turned out as could rightly have been expected of them, for, borne on by unbridled zeal, they literally "wore themselves out" physically, intellectually, and sometimes morally . . .

The month of January is a crucial month for a young priest.

In general, the first months after leaving the seminary

are excellent. He is faithful to prayer, to his visit to the Blessed Sacrament, to his spiritual reading, to his program of studies.

But the fatigue following the feast of Christmas, the receipts or supplementary mail on the occasion of the first of January, the more vigorous cold of full winter, all these things make the observance of all the points of his rule more difficult. It is indeed rare if he is not tempted to relax a little more at this time.

A warning is sufficient to put you on your guard and to reassure you.

It is well said that though the seminary is irreplaceable for the basic formation it assures, it cannot suffice for everything. Indeed, there is a practical understanding and a shade of meaning which only experience can give.

Conclusions:

1. Accept humbly the idea that you do not know everything (there is no dishonor in that).

2. Do not be trenchant or absolute in your judgments.

3. Have a certain deference for your seniors; do not judge them, but seek their advice.

4. By seeking their advice, you will better understand the reasons which have escaped you for such and such a manner of acting; and, in any case, you will act with better understanding of the cause. (I should add here: and, you will gain their sympathy.)

5. Especially in the first year, do not seek so much to do better than "that which is being done," as to do "that which is being done" as well as you can.

Be faithful to your mental prayer. Make your preparation

the night before. But do not spread out your spiritual life. Center it on the Mass and the breviary. What admirable subjects for prayer will you find in the missal and in the psalms!

Look upon prayer not as a conscientious reading of a meditation book, but as a drawing aside for an intimate and intense contact with God who lives in you. He desires to give himself to you with his light and his power, and this in the measure in which you give yourself to him with all your trust and all your love. The purpose of prayer is that you be a little more impregnated by the divine, that you have in your spirit a little more of the thoughts of Jesus Christ, in your heart a little more of his sentiments, in your will a little more of his divine strength, in all your being a little more of his grace, in such a manner that no one can approach you without sensing that there is in you something other than yourself: Jesus Christ, whom you must serve with the "increase of humanity."

The ideal will be to say the hours of your breviary at the corresponding hours of the day: Lauds at dawn, Terce around 9:00, Sext around noon, None in the afternoon, Vespers before supper, Compline (and Matins of the following day) before going to bed. But if experience shows that you cannot keep this schedule, recite your breviary *quam primum moraliter* in the spirit of each hour.

Do not forget that the breviary is essentially a community prayer. As often as possible, say it with another priest. If you live in a community and a part of the breviary is recited in common, profit by it and be scrupulously faithful in being there to participate. Recall the words of our Lord:

"When two or three of you shall be gathered together in my name, anything you ask shall be given you."

Be careful to remember in reciting your breviary all the souls entrusted to you, and to pray in their name.

There is no prayer in the world more powerful than that of the whole Christ said officially to the Father in heaven by our consecrated lips. The more charity you put into the recitation of your breviary, the more your breviary will make charity grow in you.

"The psalms," says Dr. Willam, "are prayers full of mystery. They dry up until they truly become a corpse when we recite them with a dry heart; they animate and furnish most edifying thoughts when we recite them with an elevated heart and take these thoughts as bases for prayer."

Let holy Mass be the sun of your priestly life. Is it not the oblation of your life completely given over into that of Christ to vivify in one all the souls of the entire world, especially those bound to you?

Begin Mass exactly at the appointed hour, and without scruple make full use of the half-hour you rightfully have to say it. Never agree to hurry through it, even under the pretext of charity toward the faithful, a false pretext, for nothing is less edifying to the Christian people than a priest who celebrates precipitously.

Reserve for yourself, in accord with the wishes of your pastor, a complete day of recollection and prayer in which you can make a monthly retreat. As often as possible, make it away from the parish, far from the usual place of your occupations. The ideal would be a monastery or a seminary, or, if nothing better is available, the rectory of a friend, but someplace where you can be sure of the needed hours of silence.

If priestly retreats are organized in a fruitful manner, that is, with time provided for recollection, be sure to take part in them regularly. And should an important reason in your ministry prevent you from going, make up for it as soon as possible; in the active life of today's ministry, the monthly retreat is both a right and a necessity for the young priest.

During these days of recollection, reread your notes from your ordination retreat and the program of your spiritual life. Make an account of your resolutions and of your progress. Take note of the points that need special work. Prepare some subjects for mental prayer to use during the month. Take cognizance of your confession and spiritual direction.

Go to confession regularly. "Every two weeks" seems to be a good mean; once a month, a minimum. The ideal is that your confessor be at the same time a true director to whom you can speak freely, without reticence, one from whom you can receive judicious counsel, stimulating exactingness, and paternal control.

From the intellectual as well as the spiritual point of view, do not be content with what you got in the seminary. This is the place to recall these two axioms: "He who does not advance falls backward," and "Stagnation is death." Indeed, you have received such an abundance of light and grace in your formative years that you can live on your reserves for three or four years. But if you do not take stock, you will soon be like the capitalist who eats up all his capital: you will soon find that you have nothing to give and that you have become incapable of personal thought.

Have always on hand some fundamental spiritual reading. Such are the works of the fathers, or great authors whether ancient or modern. But do not be content to read for the sake of reading. There is no true intellectual work unless there is assimilation, and no assimilation is possible without personal reaction. So read actively, whether by making summaries, or by noting interesting references, or by writing out the most striking passages, or better yet—by trying, with the book closed, to write down for yourself what you have retained and comparing this with the original.

File your work and your notes. *The memory is a faculty for forgetting*, says Father Gratry, and, without exception, after a few years you will remember but vaguely such and such a sentence that struck you from such and such a book that interested you.

However, the important thing is not the classifying of your notes, but being able to find them again easily.

In classifying, distinguish clearly between works and notes. Sermon plans, conferences, dissertations, review articles are to be filed in vertical or horizontal folders indexed according to your personal cataloging system.

On the other hand, it may be profitable to write such things as the brief notes from your reading and various brief citations in a copy book or large notebook as you go along, one after the other. Indicate precisely the exact reference (the name of the author of the book, the edition and the page) and mention as well the date on which you took the notes. When you have filled the notebook, you can make an index according to authors or according to subjects.

The great advantage of this method is this:

1. These notes will be in less danger of being lost than if they were in a file where they would be consulted only rarely (unless it concerns work in hand on a definite subject).

2. The very fact of having assembled them in a notebook makes it easier to find them and exercises your visual memory, especially if you are careful to page through them once in a while.

3. Through rereading them and finding them again and again in the same place, they tend to become a part of you, and you will cite them and will be inspired by them without any effort at research.

Keep everything in good order. Recall the principle: *a place for everything and everything in its place; a time for everything and everything in its time.*

Let the furniture in your room and your study be practical and modest. Do not hesitate to make the necessary outlays for a file cabinet or a library, but avoid all useless luxury. Make of your room neither a museum nor a boudoir. A note of virile austerity befits a priest who, by his life even more than by his words, should preach Jesus Christ crucified.

Keep your accounts in order. Do not mix your personal money with other funds. Keep strict record of your Masses.

Make it a point of honor never to have debts. Do not let bills wait; paying them by return mail immediately is the best way to avoid needless worry.

Never lend money without having asked the advice of an experienced confrere:

1. It is difficult for you to realize how many young priests let themselves be easily moved by professional exploiters of priestly charity.

2. Quite often, money lent is money lost, and, we might add, friendship lost, for he who cannot repay feels embarrassed before his creditor and instinctively turns from him.

On the other hand, be very detached from money. May no one ever be able to accuse you of preoccupation with money. Nothing alienates souls from a priest more than the impression of dealing with a "money man."

Do not worry about money; you will never lack it for your work if you know how to give generously. It can be said without any attempt at paradox: money will come to you in the measure in which you do not go after it.

Think often of the versicle from Ecclesiasticus which the Church has us say in the office of confessors: "Happy the man found without fault, and who has not turned aside after gold, nor has he placed his hope in money and in riches. Who is he, that we may praise him? for in his life he has done wonders."

2 RELATIONS WITH THE PASTOR

Consider it a great grace to begin the first years of your priestly life under the direction of a pastor who may be for you both a father and a boss.

You have to admit that on leaving the seminary, even if you were the leader in your class, you have a good deal yet to learn. Only experience in the parish ministry can give you a practical knowledge of pastoral life. But this experience is all the more fruitful when it is directed, especially in the beginning, by a pastor who accepts being both your mentor and your guide.

Meditate on these principles:

1. Your pastor will impart to you his experience more easily and more willingly if you ask his counsel.

2. Your pastor will act like a devoted father toward you inasmuch as you conduct yourself like an attentive son.

3. Your pastor will put confidence in you to the extent that, by your loyalty, your fidelity, your spirit of faith, your humility, your ardent but disinterested zeal, you show yourself worthy.

There is usually a considerable difference in age between you and your pastor. You belong to two different generations, and it is inevitable that you will not always see things in the same light or feel the same about them. It will be the same for you later on with your curates, when you will in your turn be a pastor.

Do not let these little differences bother you; they are quite natural. Strive first to understand the thoughts of the one in charge.

Certainly you have the right respectfully to state the value of your point of view, but it will more likely be accepted if you have first understood that of your pastor.

Never forget that the final decision rests with the pastor. You are not in charge of this parish, but at this parish of which the pastor has charge. (There is a difference.)

You are like an extension of the pastor. He has the final responsibility before God and the bishop for the souls and the conduct of the parish. He has the care and the charge (curam).

Be most respectful to your pastor. Both interiorly and exteriorly, show him all the respect to which he has a right as your leader and as leader of the Christian community. Even if he admits you little by little into his intimacy, do not let your respectfulness fall down.

If Father is already advanced in age, he may suffer from infirmities which influence his character. As you have your faults, he can have his. It is not for you to judge. Remember the episode of Noah and his sons. Apply to yourself the maxim of St. Augustine: "Neque indignari, neque flere, sed intelligere."

Make it an absolute rule of conduct never to criticize your pastor. This does not mean just before your parishioners—that goes without saying, and by breaking that rule you would be committing a grave psychological as well as moral fault—but it applies also in the company of your confreres.

If, at times, you find it necessary to get it off your chest, do it before your spiritual director or your major seminary rector. These are men of experience and counsel. But do not seek consolation or support among the members of your natural or spiritual family. Such would be the ultimate blunder and imprudence.

If a dark cloud one day rises between you and Father— and this can happen even in the most fervent rectories as in the best of homes—do not embitter the affair by a sulky attitude or by resentment. Try to smooth out misunderstandings with a humble explanation. If it seems too difficult or inopportune, silently and generously accept the little passing suffering that may result, and do not take it hard.

Some good advice: force yourself, at the first opportunity, to say something good about Father, e.g.: "Father is very good with the poor," or "Father gave a good sermon Sunday." The first effect of saying something good about him with conviction will be to calm yourself. Secondly, since there is every reason to think word of it will get back to him, an easing of tensions may follow and the air will be quickly cleared.

Consider your first three years of the ministry an apprenticeship. Accept advice and even a little control. This is not a lack of confidence, but it is in your interest and the interest of souls.

If Father criticizes you on some point, perhaps about your sermon, take it in good spirits and thank him sincerely. If you do not, perhaps he will not care to do so

again for fear of making things hard for you, and this will
be a great loss for you.

Later, you will see that it takes more courage to make
such a remark to a subordinate than to receive one from a
superior.

Seek the advice of your pastor beforehand. For example:
you have a sermon to prepare, a children's retreat to preach.
Propose your plan to him and ask bibliographical suggestions. After the sermon, ask for his criticism.

Do not take any important initiative without speaking to
him about it. The more confidence he places in you, the
more you must take it to heart to keep him informed.

Here is a detail which seems secondary to some, but
which can have important consequences: be scrupulous
about punctuality, whether it be for your morning Mass,
or for other duties (especially burials), or as well for your
meals if you eat with the pastor. Punctuality is of primary
importance in priestly politeness.

Sometimes difficulties arise between pastors and curates
regarding, or rather (let us not avoid the issue) because of
the way things are run around the rectory. This may be due
to an old housekeeper who has been in the pastor's service
a long time and whose devotion has become somewhat
despotic. She may even be a relative of the pastor, and this,
needless to say, makes the case even more delicate.

Do not be surprised, but be realistic . . . and diplomatic.
Without entrusting confidences to them, and without let-
ting them get involved in things not their business, give
these people the respect due their age, their devotion, or
their kinship. You will verify again the well known maxim

of St. Francis de Sales: "*You can catch more flies with a spoon of honey than with a barrel of vinegar.*"

You should relish praying with your pastor. Happy the rectory where at least part of the office is said in common each day, where conversations are frankly priestly, where there is joy in speaking with open heart of him who is our reason for living and who is each day our reason for giving without counting the cost.

Remember also to pray for Father! As curate, you have a duty to pray often to the Holy Spirit for him. Ask our Lord insistently to keep the union between your minds and hearts productive.

How can the Master who preached so much the "*sint unum*" to his apostles be deaf to such a prayer?

3 RELATIONS WITH OTHER CONFRERES

If charity is to be exercised toward all, it applies in the first
degree toward those who participate in the same priesthood. Was not the commandment most insisted upon by
our Lord that of charity among the apostles? charity even
to the extent of humble service: "*Exemplum dedi
vobis. . . .*"

We sometimes find among priests a regrettable error: they
are most zealous and charitable toward the faithful in their
care, but they seem never to have had the idea that their
closest neighbor is their brother priest.

We are not speaking of indiscreet zeal, nor of misplaced
paternalism, and even less of a reform spirit; rather we speak
of that priestly tact which makes a priest, without wishing
to impose himself, always ready to give cordial aid, fraternal
comfort to a slightly disappointed, soured or discouraged
confrere.

Can we not also say that true charity among priests, "*non
solum verbo et lingua, sed opere et veritate,*" is one of the
most efficacious means of edifying the faithful, one of the
best apologetic arguments for the unbelievers: "*In hoc cog-
noverunt omnes*"?

Again, let us not forget that our Lord considers done to
himself whatever we do to those he calls not only his serv-

ants, but his friends, even his "other selves": *"Quamdiu fecistis uni ex his fratribus, mihi fecistis."*

But, he who wounds fraternal charity will be its first victim, for our heart was made to love and to feel itself loved. We need an atmosphere of good will, mutual confidence and fraternal sympathy to develop fully.

Grace elevates nature, but it does not destroy it. It surpasses nature, but it does not pass it by. The priestly life requires the control of our affections, but it does not suppress them. By the very fact of our vocation, God has given us hearts which are more generous and more ardent. For us, fraternal charity is both a necessity and a driving force.

So let us be careful of coolness, of indifferent airs. Let us be interested in what our associates are doing, rejoice in their successes. Let us aid them with our encouragements, our active sympathy.

"Oh the noble hearts," says Father Faber, "that have succumbed beneath the depressing weight of lack of sympathy! Oh the plans for the glory of God that have fallen dead in the water for lack of a smile, or friendly encouragement!"

Let us be aware of the need to encourage our confreres. Jesus was not afraid to give encouragement: *"Euge, serve bone et fidelis."* At Gethsemani he even asked for a little encouragement and compassion for himself.

Tertullian hurled a challenge at the pagans: "See how they love one another!" he says, speaking of the Christians; and was it not this very point, "see how they love one another," that brought about so many conversions? Could it not also bring about numerous vocations in our day?

Among the priests of a parish or of neighboring parishes there is no place for rivalries, for jealousies. Let us challenge those cutting remarks which so-called well intentioned people unawaredly distort (for what does a sentence mean out of context?) and then relate to us.

If we find around us misunderstandings, we should be careful not to share in them. We can excuse ourselves on the grounds of our youth and our inexperience from ever judging and from blaming anyone whomsoever. Nor should we neglect any occasion to facilitate a favorable interpretation of things and to promote better mutual understanding. We should remain prudent and discreet, praying interiorly that priests be always united in spirit through truth and united in heart through charity.

Often, differences between confreres are more a question of form than of basics. In such a situation, do not hesitate to make as many concessions as possible *ad bonum pacis*. Recall the words of sacred Scripture: "*Responsio mollis frangit iram.*" Preserve your calm and serenity.

If, in a meeting or a reunion, your zeal carries you a little too far and you hurt a confrere, do not be slow to apologize. If, on the contrary, you are the one treated unjustly, forgive graciously and, especially, hold no grudge.

Priestly friendship has solid foundations: participation in the same eternal priesthood, the same formation under the same revered masters, the same goal, and the same mission. But we must not neglect the humble means of preserving and developing it: a few words of condolence on the occasion of a bereavement, a few lines of joyful congratulations on the occasion of a promotion, some words of sympathy during some trial, a card of thanks for a service rendered. These are the little things which solidify friendship.

Friendship should not derogate from respect; quite the contrary. And, reciprocally, mutual respect is an indispensable substratum for lasting friendships. Never forget that behind the man or the appearances of our confreres lies Christ the Sovereign Priest. If we wish the faithful to hold the priesthood in high esteem, we should seek to venerate it in the heart of all those who share in it.

Whatever may be the remembrances of college or wartime comrades, our confreres are not simply comrades. They are other Christs, and this should be sensed in the way we treat them, in the way we speak of them.

Brotherly friendship will be all the more strong and fruitful if there is a true interchange of mutual aid in all its forms: pastoral, intellectual, spiritual. May the formula "*oremus pro invicem*" not be an empty one; may the oft repeated words "united in prayer" be not simply a stylistic phrase. Every priest has a duty to pray for his brothers: "*frater adjuvatus a fratre quasi civitas firma.*"

For the good of our confreres on the same path, there will be some daily invocation: "*Virgo fidelis, ora pro nobis,*" a rendezvous at some little hour of the breviary, Terce (the hour of Pentecost) for example, or concelebration of Mass once a year, with permission if necessary.

More or less frequent gatherings (according to local possibilities) will strengthen this mutual aid.

Even if you maintain filial and confident relations with

your pastor, as is desirable, it is of course normal and perfectly legitimate to want to meet from time to time with
confreres of your own age.

From many points of view, these reunions among the
junior clergy can be profitable.

In these confraternal reunions, carefully guard against all
criticism of your seniors.

In a work entitled *Éducation et Adolescence*, Father
Rimaud very justly remarks: a noble sentiment stirs generous youths about their twenty-fifth year, the time when
they become young men; it is the social ambition to change
the world and to accomplish the good their seniors have not
done. To snuff out this sentiment would be to crush
motives, to clip wings, to tie down souls. But this ambition
is fruitful only on condition that those who take it to heart
strive first to surpass themselves, to testify by their irre-
proachable competence and by their effective dedication
that they are worthy of it.

"To listen to some young priests," a seminary superior
once said, "it would seem that the earth turns only when
their feet are on it."

Never fall into such folly; and certainly avoid any systematic criticism of your predecessors, criticism which often
does more harm to those who offer it than to those who are
its object.

It goes without saying that we must avoid criticism of the
hierarchy at all cost, and in general of all those who hold
positions of authority. You will see later that, though criticism is easy, the art of conducting things well is difficult:

ars artium regimen animarum. All criticism of authority quickly becomes an injustice, for not all the facts are known to us.

Then too, criticism of authority is most often sterile, for it usually tears down without building up. And it is always harmful, for it shuts us off from the *gratia capitis*, that precious grace of union with the head which is the condition of the divine benediction on all our activities.[1]

Regarding superiors—and each has his merits as well as his faults—remember his position of authority, and in addition, look to Jesus Christ himself. That *Promitto* should not be an empty word you responded with before the kiss of peace in the ordination ceremony when you answered the formal demand of the Pontifical: "Do you promise me and my successors reverence and obedience?" *Reverentiam et obedientiam.* First respect; it makes obedience easier and its fruit is peace.

A social body without discipline is doomed to anarchy, to decomposition, to death. The strength of a community does not depend alone on the personal strength of each member; it also depends on the cohesive force which unites all the members under their leader for a common purpose. The stronger the reign of confidence and love among all, the easier it will be to accept discipline and the more effective that discipline will be.

It is inconceivable that priests be able to get together without having occasion to speak with open hearts about him who has taken hold of their hearts. Sometimes we see

[1] On this subject, read the meditation entitled "Loyalty to Our Bishop" in *Before His Face*, volume 1, New York 1962, 175–192.

among priests an extraordinary timidity in this regard. Is this human respect with regard to peers? Is it tepidity of soul? Is it an effect of the individualism characteristic of clerical formation in certain seminaries? Is it for fear, as I once heard it said, of being called "a fanatic"?

Let us break with the exaggerated fears which can deprive one another of us of a great moral support. "We cannot refrain from speaking of him," said the apostles. Who could better interest the souls of priests gathered together than Christ who, as Gaston de Renty said, is the best cement of their friendship? In the last analysis, is he not our very reason for living, for laboring, for loving? Is he not our real center of interest? And can we not say that for the soul of the priest, all, even the ministry, makes no sense and has no value whatever if not related to him?

There is a great temptation for us to speak of our works as an industrialist speaks of his factory. The priest is the "vicem gerens Domini," and if the Lord does not have the first place in the hearts of his laborers, their labor is in vain.

It is not for us to preach to our confreres, much less to teach them a lesson. That would be indelicate and out of place. Nor are we to direct everything to a subject of piety. Good humor, joviality, pleasantries in good taste, some good stories are excellent in priestly reunions.

St. Joan did not want the bow always bent, and St. Louis wanted the religious doctors he invited to his table to be able to argue amicably over most varied subjects—and he himself felt no repugnance to these "quod libet."

It is all a question of degree, of touch, of tact. The harm will be that the playful or light tone will be the rule and that one will come away from the gathering without anything for the soul, whether with regard to an intellectual subject, the ministry, or even that "sursum corda" which stirs an impulse ad Dominum.

A conversation in which our faith and our love of Christ sincerely shine through can be, for a weary or tempted confrere, the spark to rekindle the flame.

Mutual aid can be on the intellectual level too. Do not be afraid to take an interest in the books or review articles your confreres read. Know how to ask questions, first of all to enrich yourself, but also to give your friend the joy of communicating a little of his knowledge. All this is on condition, properly understood, that there is mutual advantage.

Mutual aid can be especially exercised on the pastoral level. With your pastor's permission, invite one or another of your confreres to come and preach to children or teenagers of your parish, for an Easter retreat, for a solemn communion retreat, or for a day of recollection for group leaders. Or even have them examine the children on their catechism. See to it that you are ready to render the same service in return.

A little advice: when you have invited a confrere to preach in your parish, do not forget to thank him and to tell him of your appreciation of his sermon. Believe me, he is waiting for it, he wants it. It can be very useful to him even if, and especially if, sincerity obliges you to make a few delicate criticisms, yet does not keep you from finishing, whatever the state of the matter, with a word of encouragement.

If one day a confrere asks to go to confession to you (and

this will surely happen, perhaps at the moment when you least expect it), do not use your youth or inexperience as a pretext to shirk it. Accept with all simplicity, unite yourself closely to Jesus Christ the Sovereign Priest, and prove yourself a true brother.

Never throw a rock at a brother who is weak, and, a *fortiori*, at a brother who has fallen. Do not forget that often a fall may have excusing or attenuating causes that you do not know about. Among these causes, we must often put in first place a lack of friendship or priestly sympathy. Beyond this, as the venerable Cardinal Verdier loved to repeat: "A failure, even a grave one, can be the point of departure for a priestly life of renewed fervor, prudence and generosity, on condition that it encounters a fraternal hand, and even more a fraternal heart, to aid in remounting the slope."

For a true priest, all the aspects of the ministry are fair: catechism, visits to the poor and the sick, sermons, etc.

But none is more fair to him than aiding other priests to become more priestly.

4 RELATIONS WITH PARISHIONERS

By the word "parishioners" we do not mean only those who come to services or who take part in the movements or societies, but rather all the inhabitants of the parish, believers and unbelievers, indifferent and sympathetic. As assistant, you should share with your pastor in the concern, the care, the service of all these souls.

First, you must know your parish well, not merely its territorial geography, but also its human geography. What a passionate search! to know well those for whom you are in part responsible. This is the first condition for giving the response they have a right to hear from you, and for giving them what their souls need.

Here are some things a young priest ought to know about the parish within a few months: the history of the parish, also the history of the pastors and the priests who have preceded him, some knowledge of the economic life of the parish, and especially about the mentality of the various types of laborers.

What is the demographic evolution of the parish? How many people were here one hundred years ago, fifty years ago, before the war, now? the proportion of births and baptisms; the number of school-age children in relation to the total number of inhabitants; attendance at Sunday Mass;

the number of men at paschal services, the number of women there; the total number of communions in a year; the number of sick who have died with the sacraments in relation to those who have died without, etc.

Finally, what are the causes of indifference or impiety? Which are the principal centers of influence: the city hall, the school, the drugstore, the movie theatre, the tavern? What are the most widespread objections? What is the circulation of the city's newspapers?

This should be your dominant preoccupation: what are the needs of each of the many types of my parishioners? What does the priest need to know in order to serve them better?

Never forget what the people, even the indifferent, expect in the priest: that he be completely and uniquely a priest. "The priest," Cardinal Verdier would often repeat, "is like an eighth sacrament. He is the bearer of grace inasmuch as he acts as a priest."

Be priestly in all your life, in all your words, in your way of dealing with everyone. Thus you will verify that the priest is effective by his very presence; his contacts, whether in the course of the ministry or simply in the course of daily life, can be a source of light and life for souls.

In your manner of officiating, of saying holy Mass, of distributing holy communion, of baptizing, of blessing a grave, of saying the rosary, even of reading the announcements, show yourself sincere, and you will at times touch souls more deeply than by the most beautiful oratory of your sermons.

Be assiduous and exact. Whether it be for the hour of

Mass, the time of confessions, or for the least-important meeting, never make people wait. You cannot expect punctuality of others if you do not give the example.

Be careful of your exterior appearance. You have a perfect right to be poor—but you have an obligation to be always proper. If you do not watch yourself, you can easily become negligent on this point. If you happen to live in a community, ask one of your confreres to give you charitable reminders on this point. A priest should respect in himself—even in his exterior bearing—his priesthood, if he wants others to respect it.

In your relations with your parishioners, be neither stiff nor distant, neither ceremonious nor affected. Let your attitude be always amiable, but dignified, simple and reserved.

You certainly have much work. Never forget that you are a man of God for men, and these souls have a right over you. In their interest, reserve for yourself a few moments of silence and recollection; but, outside of this time, be always at their disposal.

Do not forget that many people are in contact with a priest only on exceptional occasions (the request for information in view of a baptism, a marriage, a funeral) and judge their parish priests according to the opinions they form of us at these moments. If they are well received, and if, in addition, they are edified by our manner of explaining and carrying out the ceremonies, they will take away a favorable impression that will one day facilitate a return visit.

Be kind, patient and understanding with the poor, and

in general with all the people. With the great, the powerful, the rich, be respectful—it is not good to affront them —but remain dignified and independent.

Be aware of the timidity of many people when they cross the threshold of a sacristy. For those who are infrequently at church, their impressionableness is extreme. A pleasant expression, a word of encouragement can lead them back toward God, just as, on the contrary, a rude or a grumpy word can alienate them for a very long time.

Being reserved does not mean being distant or haughty. The people have a saying which seems to sum up the conditions for their confidence: "One thing about Father so and so, he is not stuck up"—which is to say, he is simple, good, he does not put on airs; we like to talk to him.

Always and everywhere be a priest, even with those with whom you do business. Certainly you are not to be naive, but, as St. Francis Xavier says: "The conversion of souls is more important than the maintaining of our rights, and besides, these latter were given us only to serve the good of the former."

Take reasonable care of your reputation, but avoid going to extremes which will make you the object of ridicule. At one time it was frowned upon to see priests in public in the company of women; now we are liberated, of course, from these Victorian restrictions. In your relations with women, however, be prudent and use your common sense; and as a general rule, perhaps, avoid being seen in public too often with any one particular young woman—innocent and pastoral as the relationship may be.

Do not avoid political or social discussion, whether in private or in public. But remember that many times your parishioners might take your private opinions to be the "official" opinion of the Church. Healthy discussion of pressing social problems such as civil rights or aid to the poor will do much to bring you into more direct, involved contact with your parishioners. They will respond much more freely to you if they know you are interested in their problems, in the crucial social problems of the community and nation. Remember the great hope of Pope John, the vision of *aggiornamento*, that the Church and all her people —priests included—find greater commitment in secular life. We have been asked to open the windows of the Church; let us not tarry in opening the windows of our rectories.

Be most prudent in your conversations (both public and private) about all that concerns your parishioners. Do not talk about your faithful even to the members of your family. There is a certain professional secrecy of the priest even beyond that of the confessional. Your observations can, passing from mouth to mouth, return more or less distorted to the ears of the persons concerned. And if the reports are unfavorable, they can cause you difficulties, grave difficulties; and, if they are favorable, they can rouse jealousies.

Let your discretion be proverbial; nobody will reproach you for being circumspect. People's confidence in you depends to a great part on your reputation from this point of view. In the archaic language of the official acts of the middle ages the name of a priest often appears together

with these words: "A discreet and knowledgeous person."
The priest is one who knows many things and knows how
to discern what to say and what not to.

A priest naturally needs money for the work he has to do
and the poor he has to help. He is led to put out his hand,
but let it be only for the Church. Often he must even seek
benefactors. Do this with tact, dignity, disinterestedness.
On the other hand, when you receive, know how to say
thank you simply and unaffectedly.

Your relations with your parishioners can be summed up
in the following manner: the ideal is that all will be led
to sense in you the priest, above all, Jesus Christ, and in
hearing you speak, in seeing you act, they can say in all
truth: "Yes, it is indeed as Christ spoke and acted."

5 THE YOUNG PRIEST AND PREACHING

Nos autem . . . ministerio verbi instantes erimus. The apostles considered the apostolate of the word, conjoined with that of prayer, the first of their ministrations. The preaching of the priest is the ordinary channel through which God transmits grace and light to the Christian community.

Look upon preaching as the expression, in a given age and in a given usage, of the Gospel message which, by virtue of the sacrament of order, it is our mission to transmit to the world in the very name of the holy Trinity.

Always have a high regard for this ministry of the word. If it is true to say that the personal element has its place here (it is perhaps here, of all the forms of priestly ministry, that action "ex *opere operantis*" has the most important role), we must never forget that the "sermon" is not simply a human speech. It is the word of God making use of a man "consecrated" for the very purpose of bearing witness to the truth and communicating authentically in his behalf.

In preparing your sermons, be on guard against two extremes: too hasty a preparation which leaves you to mount the pulpit without the care and time to master your subject, and too careful a preparation which is out of proportion with your other obligations in the ministry.

However, in the very first years of your priestly life, it is in your interest to dedicate more time to this than in the following years.

Is it necessary to memorize your sermons? Certainly not. You will be bound by your text; you will not be yourself. In spite of all your efforts, it will influence the lesson delivered, will rob you of that spontaneity so necessary for audience contact. The more your memory—the faculty of forgetting —is fallible, the more you risk those lapses which are so difficult for the audience as well as for the speaker.

Before mounting the pulpit, know most exactly how you will begin and how you will finish. Have your outline well in mind. And, united to God, launch out heartily.

Must you write every sermon? During the first years, it would be wise. This is the best way to make yourself compose, limit your sentences, enrich your vocabulary. But once your sermon is written, make yourself a detailed outline. This outline will let you speak *ex abundantia cordis*, while all the time knowing where you are going.

In the preparation of your sermon, as in its delivery, never lose sight of your audience. Do not ask yourself: "What do I want to tell them?" but: "What do they need to know? What will they understand and accept? What should they be reminded of? What will their reactions be to my exhortations and advice?"

A psychological understanding of the audience is the first condition for contact with them. It is essential not only that the word goes forth, but also that the word produces. It is essential not only that the people hear, but also that they understand and assimilate.

Whether your subject is assigned to you or is of your free choice, begin by reflecting, seeing your audience in advance, sensing the needs of their souls. Ask yourself what ideas must pass into their spirits, what sentiments must be made to pulse in their hearts.

Do not be afraid to go down on your knees whether in the church or before your crucifix. The better sermons are the prayed sermons. "To preach," says St. Thomas Aquinas, is "*contemplata aliis tradere.*" Offer yourself to the divine Master that he may send you the Spirit of truth, that you may grow in wisdom and grace.

Then, at your table, write down on paper the thoughts that have presented themselves to you.

The day will come when, with experience, your learning from studies and reading, and your prayer life, you will be able to construct a well-rounded and workable outline fairly rapidly.

In the beginning, if you lack ideas, you might base your sermon outline on an article on liturgy, or ecumenism or Scripture that appears in one of the magazines you subscribe to; or you might read the sermons or devotional writings of such great preachers as Cardinal Newman, or John Donne or St. Ignatius of Loyola. And there is abundant sermon material in the encyclicals and allocutions of such popes as Pius XII, John XXIII or Paul VI, or in such decrees of the Second Vatican Council as *The Constitution on the Sacred Liturgy.* Let these inspire you to make your own outline; but do not give in to the temptation to copy someone else's sermon.

Fill out your outline with citations or examples. This

is where your own notes can be of great service to you and can give your preaching an original attractiveness. Use a maximum of sacred Scripture. Do not forget that the inspired words have a power all their own. But avoid when you can Latin quotes, and, if you use any, never fail to translate them.

One of the great temptations for the young preacher is to wish to say everything without going deeply into anything. It is necessary to know how to select. Have no more than two or three ideas in a sermon, and come to practical and clear conclusions which can be easily retained and immediately assimilated.

If you have the good fortune to have near you a pastor or older confrere, show him your sermon outline and ask his advice. Or ask the advice of a priest who is your own age. The experience of others, especially elders, can be very enriching.

The night before, or at least sometime before mounting the pulpit, go over your sermon mentally.

When the moment comes to speak, offer yourself to our Lord that it may be he who speaks through your lips, and offer him your listeners that it may be he who hears in their hearts.

Many preachers, often among the best, have experienced stage fright. You, too, will experience it. Do not be surprised or disturbed. Ask the help of Mary and of your guardian angel. You can be almost sure that your timidity will disappear once your sermon is begun.

Before beginning your sermon, look at your entire audience; take note of the long rows of people. Do not forget that you are speaking to them. Do not lose sight of them if you want to be in contact with them.

Be careful not to give all your voice at the beginning. Articulate clearly, without exaggeration. Adapt your delivery to the number of your listeners. Speak slowly, vary the tone. Especially avoid final monotones and cadences. Strive to be lively and natural.

Especially in the first years, do not seek to play the great orator. Avoid using rhetorical sentences solely for effect.

Do not put on a solemn air. If God has endowed you with true oratorical talent, it will show itself with the years, on condition that you have worked hard in the beginning and that you have strived for simplicity.

Facility can pose a great danger for the young priest, for, though it aids him to gain some success, it can deceive him. He will not work hard enough; he will little by little take on the faults of those who speak without saying anything; he will become a "tinkling cymbal."

To make your sermons more alive, converse mentally with your listeners, and even explicitly offer them interruptions: "But perhaps you think that . . . You might be tempted to say to me . . . I can imagine what you are thinking . . ." Call upon their experience, their memory, their heart: "Have you not observed that . . . ?" Do not hesitate to question them: "What do you think of this way of . . . ? Tell me: was not our divine Lord right?"

Sometimes certain preachers give the impression that they are so preoccupied with their subject and with the enchantment of their ideas that they have forgotten their hearers. They speak before their audience, not to it.

Do not fall into the error of those preachers who, once in the pulpit, seem to be in another world: "I speak. Let him understand who can, let him accept who will."

Relate what you say to the life of your hearers. Make reference to one of their real and immediate preoccupations. Bring to mind some reflection they themselves have had, or which they, like you, have accepted as part of life. Evoke their cares, their objections, their fears. In a word, according to the concise phrase of Father Lacordaire, go "to the heart of the situation" of your hearers.

Use correct English in a pleasing tone, but without artificiality. Be neither vulgar nor prissy.

Guard against professional strictures: avoid overly technical terms. If you use technical terms, explain them if necessary.

There are also venerable expressions in the translations of the Scriptures or the liturgy which must be retranslated, because they are outdated; for example: "He who confesses me before men, him also will I confess before my Father," or "It is consummated." Ask yourself what such expressions mean to your people. Always watch them and their reactions to see the effect.

Speak as an apostle, not as a professor or a lawyer. You are not there to teach a college course or to plead a legal case. You are there to bring into the hearts of your hearers the faith you live, the flame that burns in you.

"If we are not burning with love, others around us will perish in the cold" (Mauriac).

Today's generations are not so much in need of apologetic discussions as they are of the living and life-giving revelation of the Christian message. Today's work is not to prove the existence of God or the divinity of Christ, but to put our finger on the present needs of Christ among us. As the catechetical renewal has made so clear, we must bring to our people the kerygma, the "good news of salvation." We must proclaim the saving action of Jesus our Redeemer, and help our people to be living witnesses to the truth of the Gospel.

This is the hour for ardent lives lifted by a powerful and true mystique; it is the time for living testimony.

Extend your horizons as far as possible. Do not limit the end of life to the question of personal salvation. Here, among others, are some ideas you can return to again and again:

—God knows us and loves us personally. He calls us in an existential manner, asking all of us to live in a communion of charity—the very communion in which the Father, the Son and the Holy Spirit live united—and to realize this union by allowing men to participate in the life of the Son made man.

—The liturgy is the cult of the Mystical Body of Christ, that is, of the Head and of the members. It is the privileged place of an actual encounter between God and man in our Lord.

—By baptism and confirmation, we are made witnesses of Jesus Christ.

—We are not here on earth to live in isolation, but to live in community. We are part of a great community called the Church, and we are to pray, work, rejoice, suffer in a community spirit.

—The priesthood of the faithful: "The layman, who by his baptism and confirmation in Christ the Priest is a consecrated person, should offer himself with him and in him and through him" (Bishop Emile Joseph de Smedt).

—Perfection is the work of Christ himself living in us by faith. It is the full life of charity perfected by the gifts of the Spirit (Thomas Merton).

—The greatest commandment is that of charity. It does not consist only in giving alms and refraining from scandal. It is an active participation in the charity of God himself for men. "Charity is much more than a duty, much more than an exercise of virtue. It is an essential function of the supernatural life" (Abbe Long Masselmans).

—We are not here on earth to have a tranquil life so much as a productive life.

—Without God, we can do nothing. We have a great need of him. But he has pushed delicateness to the point of desiring to need us. He made us not just his creatures, his servants, his children, but his collaborators. He takes this collaboration seriously.

—We are not on the earth just to save our souls and preserve them from hell, but to work with Jesus Christ to spiritualize humanity and to save the world.

—We are not responsible only for the evil that we do, but also for the good we did not do, through carelessness or laziness.

—The same Christ lives in each of us, and considers the good or evil we do to others done also to himself.

Speak with conviction. Avoid exaggerated and grandiloquent airs, but let your words convey the fact that these truths you preach are truths you live by and are willing to die for.

"It is easy to preach the Gospel without risk. The most vibrant eloquence remains inoffensive. Only the word of one who bases his life on the words of Christ is capable of striking decisive blows" (Canon Thellier of Poncheville).

Faith is contageous in proportion to its intensity. A priest never has a right to speak of religious things with an air of detachment. There is a way of speaking of Christ which will let your hearers know that, for you, Jesus is not a neutral or far-away being, but Someone living, the great Friend who has taken possession of your heart.

Be *kind*. Let everything, in your expression, in your attitude, in your tone of voice, reflect kindness. Before even beginning to make the sign of the cross, envelop your audience in a great act of charity: "If you only knew how much I love you and how much I want to help you to make Christ increase in you." Try it. You will be surprised how quickly you will win the sympathy and confidence of your listeners.

Besides, one reaps only what he sows, and in return you will feel encouraged and more at ease.

Be tactful. Never allow yourself to involve in personalities, not even unobliging allusions against anyone. Do not imitate those preachers who cannot mount the pulpit without assuming a fierce or irritated air. Never let yourself fall into the all too frequent fault of castigating the absent.

The day may come when you have some hard truths to speak. *Durus est hic sermo.* God demands that we be the salt of the earth, not the honey. But, the harder the message you have to deliver, the more you must use tact and kindness.

Be brief. This means: 1. Do not go beyond the time provided by the Mass schedule or the pastor. 2. Be so interesting that your listeners will say "Already!" when you leave the pulpit. You will learn to tell how this time varies according to the audience, and according to the preacher.

Have your conclusion well in mind. Do not be like the novice aviators who make many passes at the ground without landing.

If you see that your audience is tired, do not persist; that would be the wrong course. Make it short; end with a brief story or a practical conclusion relevant to them, and leave the pulpit.

It is an excellent practice, before putting away your sermon notes, to look them over again in view of some future time, to underline some forgotten passages, to add some thought that came to mind in the course of the sermon, to note some judicious remark you may have heard.

It is legitimate for you to want to know what others thought of your preaching. It is a good idea to seek friendly and constructive criticism from your pastor or a confrere. But do not become ridiculous and discuss everything about your sermon, or downgrade it, or make known the subtlety of your outline, or explain that you forgot the best passages.

And if nobody makes any comment, accept this humbly. You said what you had to say as well as you could. It is finished; it will not come back. The important thing now is that, in the intimacy of souls, our Lord makes himself known to each. Uniting yourself to his action in their hearts is your best way to make the modest grain you have sown produce in good percentage.

6 THE YOUNG PRIEST
AND THE CONFESSIONAL

Love the confessional. Aside from holy Mass, it is there that you are most a priest.

"A priest who does not love the confessional is a priest who does not love souls," says St. Alphonsus Liguori.

Be exact and assiduous. Even if there is nobody there, be at your confessional at the scheduled time. You can say your breviary or your rosary, make your visit to the Blessed Sacrament, or do your spiritual reading, but be there at the precise time scheduled. Fidelity to your choice post, the confessional, will not be without recompense. One day or another, it will result in miraculous and unexpected returns.

Before entering the confessional, invoke the Holy Spirit and turn to Jesus Christ; in his name you will listen to the penitents, enlighten them, comfort them, absolve them.

While they are telling you their sins and faults, communicate in the charity of Jesus and unite yourself to his present prayer for each of them.

In the case of a newcomer, one of the first questions to ask is: "How long has it been since your last confession?" This will already let you know what kind of soul you are communicating with.

If it is someone who has not come for a long time or if you sense some hesitancy, say a few words of encouragement such as: "Remember that I am here in our Lord's name to help you and to pardon you."

In general, let your penitents confess their sins without interruption. Intervene only to help them if you see they are embarrassed, or to encourage them if they seem nervous.

Never show surprise, not even by an exclamation, even less by remarks such as: "How could a soul like you do such a thing as that!"

Be patient. The more you are pressed, the more you must be calm. The least bruskness can turn away a soul forever. There are timorous souls who open up with difficulty; there are scrupulous souls who are always afraid of not telling enough and who never finish. If they continue to come to you, you may be able to educate them little by little, but begin by placing them in an atmosphere of confidence.

You must educate the consciences of your penitents tactfully. Confession is an instrument of mercy and should never be an instrument of torture. Remember that the Church does not demand material integrity, but formal and subjective integrity.

Treat souls with infinite respect, taking into account that the moral responsibilities of each are different.

In medicine, they often say that: "There are no sicknesses, but only sick people." We also can rightly say: "There are no sins, but only sinners."

Every case of conscience is a special case, and, as the

moral professor loved to repeat, "a battlefield of principles."

Your attitude should be summed up in three words: understanding, firmness, kindness.

Understanding: the difficulties proper to each soul, the good will already shown by the penitent's presence in the confessional, the more or less hidden good desires which must be revealed to him and made to operate for the good of his heart.

Firmness: on the principles it is not good to explain fearfully, but in such a way as to guide our conduct and direct our decisions; firmness to stimulate the soul, to help it raise itself, to strengthen itself if need be, and to surpass itself.

Kindness: which will be the expression of the Good Shepherd's charity with regard to his lost or only wounded sheep.

After the accusation of faults, interrogate only with discretion and tact. Never ask questions out of curiosity. Ask only what you need to know to judge with an understanding of the causes and to give opportune advice with certain knowledge. Scale your questions to the religious instruction and moral formation of your penitents. Take into account their possible susceptibilities. Be more ready to abstain from questioning than to ask a question that could do harm or be misinterpreted.

If the confession has not provided enough to judge the penitent, here are a few questions you might ask to delve a little deeper:

1. All together, how many times have you received holy

communion? 2. Did you make any resolution at your last confession? 3. What point would you like to work on now to please our Lord?

What often tries young confessors is sins against the sixth and ninth commandments. On this subject, there are two extremes to avoid: we must be neither shocked nor resigned—we must not take them as tragic, neither must we condone them.

This is not the place for a course in moral theology, nor for one in pastoral, but some therapeutic suggestions for the cure of this flow of bad habits may be of service.

1. Without being dramatic, take your penitent seriously. Except in pathological cases of high frequency, consider his sinful habit curable.

The first thing to seek from the penitent is the desire for a cure; the second is faith in the possibility of a cure; the third is the energetic will to take the means necessary to cure the habit.

Among these means there are supernatural ones like recourse to Christ and Mary or a frequenting of the Eucharist for at least a few weeks. However, do not forget the principle that grace surpasses nature but does not pass it by. Means of the supernatural order are of no avail without the means of the natural order.

Among the means of the natural order, there are three which must be employed together to win a definitive victory:

1. development of the inhibitive sense;
2. positive and progressive auto-suggestion;

3. a goal capable of marshaling the better activities of the soul.

Development of the inhibitive sense: what happens most of the time with the habitual sinner is the passage from idea to act without effective resistance. He must be helped to re-educate his will, especially in the area in which it has the aptitude for cutting short. Fortunately, we are able to influence the soul by showing that it is perfectly capable of self-mastery. This we do by proposing that it prove itself by a practice of simple and easy little acts of vigilance, but whose multiplication will give it confidence in its possibilities and the increased energy to avoid the particular temptation.

Positive and progressive auto-suggestion: This is one of the cases where the "Coué method" succeeds best. The penitent who agrees to repeat for some weeks, many times a day, formulas like these: "I have more and more will power; I am more and more calm; with God's grace I will be more and more the master of myself," will implant in himself psychological dispositions to facilitate victory.

A marshaling goal: This victory will be the more assured the more the penitent has a goal that will stir his enthusiasm: a soul to save, an act of charity to accomplish, an apostolic mission to realize, a good cause to serve, preparation for a Christian family. The important thing is that he not be discouraged, but take up the battle valiantly with joy and confidence.

By this method, except for pathological cases where there is a more complicated question, the most rebellious habits, granted the loyalty and generosity of the penitent, can be cured.

What is to be then recommended is the habit of a spirit of sacrifice to maintain the tone of the will. To be always prepared to cut short the desire of a forbidden pleasure, it is necessary to know to give up legitimate pleasures once in a while.

Sometimes you will encounter scrupulous souls. Scruples are not just a troubling malady, but a dangerous one. It results not from sinning, but from the inability to assure oneself of not having sinned. It is characterized by that phenomenon of repeated examinations which bring the soul to pose the same problems over and over again. This results in such a demand upon memory, reflection and concentration that the net result is mental exhaustion. It results in a paralyzing obsession, which leads to disgust for things religious, or, by way of reaction, to a disconcerting laxism. Scrupulosity in some advanced stages can become a pathological state which can be dealt with only in psychiatry.

Be firm, clear and approachable with these souls. Forbid them to go over the past, and do not hesitate to use strong words such as: "I take everything on myself, all your faults whether well or poorly confessed, and in the name of the Lord I give you his divine pardon. From now on, you are to begin a new life." Then direct the efforts of the scrupulous to positive efforts, especially in the order of charity.

In general, strive to have your penitents make practical and positive resolutions. Do not hypnotize them on the more or less deceptive negative elements. Seek to obtain progress in frequent communion—and especially a better understanding of the Mass and communion. Insist on the meaning of the state of grace, intimacy with God, the Christian meaning of duty to state and social responsibilities, the meaning of the apostolate and the duty of Catholic social action.

Avoid "stereotyped" pious exhortations. Take the trouble to adapt your advice to the needs, aspirations and abilities of each penitent.

With passing penitents, Easter penitents and children, assure yourself more of the interior act of contrition than the word-for-word recitation of the formula. For those who do not know the formula or have forgotten it, invent a short one they can repeat sentence by sentence after you, such as: "My God, I am very sorry for having offended you. Pardon all my sins. I promise to try not to commit them again. With all my heart, I want to love you. Help me be faithful to you and to please you in all circumstances."

Refuse absolution only with sure knowledge and secure conscience. If there is the slightest doubt, solve it in favor of the penitent. In certain cases, the refusal of absolution can be a salutary blow; in others, it can be a deep wound. In any case, the refusal must not be brutal. Explain it with much kindness and let the penitent know how difficult it is for you. Let your last word be always a word of encouragement, leaving the door open for better dispositions.

Vary your sacramental penances. Do not feel obliged to always give three Hail Marys. Adapt them to the strength, needs and abilities of your penitent. In some cases, it may be salutary to impose an afflictive penance, like the privation for a determined time of tobacco, alcohol, movies. Sometimes, with generous souls, especially after a grave fall, you can ask the penitent himself: "What would you like to do as a penance?" and if the proposal is reasonable, you can ratify it and give it the character of a supernatural penance.

Preserve absolute discretion in whatever has to do with your ministry in the confessional. Even aside from confessional secrecy properly so-called, avoid speaking of your penitents. Thus, do not say that Mr. Jones is your spiritual child. This is nobody's business.

You will find yourself faced with embarrassing cases of conscience on which you would like clarification. You have the perfect right to pose a question, without mentioning names, to your confessor or to one of your old seminary professors. But do not expose your case at the rectory table *coram publico*, or in front of confreres who might recognize from the given facts the person concerned.

The more you are advised to be charitable in your visits to the poor and to the sick, the more you should realize that it is a rule of good sense never to give alms in the confessional. You will risk a flood of pseudo-penitents who use the pretext of confession only to seek your pity. This can lead to a sacrilegious abuse of the sacrament.

In the confessional, do not be just a dispenser of absolution, but an educator of consciences and a real director of souls. And do not let yourself believe that it takes too much time to give stimulating and enlightening direction to souls. A few questions on resolutions taken or to be taken, on points of prayer or spiritual reading, on the subject chosen for a particular examen, on the accomplishment of duties to state in life—these do not generally demand much time and are most often quite sufficient. As a general rule, try not to give direction outside of the confessional.

Have faith in the value of frequent confession. Do not forget that the sacramental grace of absolution includes not only the grace of purification, but the right to all the actual graces useful in effectively battling the faults which caused the confessed sins.

The encyclical *Mystici Corporis* insists on the value of frequent confession:

To advance with growing ardor in the way of truth, we must give lively recommendation to the pious practice, introduced by the Church under the impulse of the Holy Spirit, of frequent confession. It augments true self-knowledge, favors Christian humility, tends to uproot bad habits, combats spiritual negligence and tepidity, purifies the conscience, fortifies the will, prepares for spiritual direction, and, as the proper effect of the sacrament, augments grace. Therefore, let those who among the younger clergy belittle the esteem for frequent confession know that theirs is a work quite contrary to the Spirit of Christ and quite deadly to the Mystical Body of our Savior.

Detachment is one of the essential qualities of the confessor. These souls do not belong to us. Above all, respect their liberty. If they leave us, let us not show surprise or resentment.

If our confessional is often frequented, let us not boast of the number of our penitents, nor of the hours spent in the tribunal of penitence. This would be a puerile vanity the Master would not bless.

If, on the contrary, our confreres have a more numerous

following, let us never take offense. Nothing is more opposed to the true apostolic spirit than jealousy, even if it is colored in the name of zeal. Is not the essential thing that the good be done? So, let us rejoice in the good done by our fellow priests: *dum omni modo Christus annuntietur.*

7 THE YOUNG PRIEST AND THE APOSTOLATE TO THE SICK

The apostolate to the sick is always a little frightening to the young priest. "How will I be received? . . . Am I going to know how to go about it?" Indeed, never allow yourself to shirk it; it is one of the essential elements of your ministry. It is here that one feels the greatest need of being helped, inspired by the Savior himself; and you can be sure his grace will not be lacking.

Share the pastor's concern to be aware of all the sick and infirm in the parish. Often the nursing sisters will furnish you with an address. Do not wait for the relatives to come and tell you. Generally, when they call a priest it is already too late. In your sermons, instructions and exhortations in the sacrament of penance, give your faithful a sense of their responsibility toward the sick. Make them understand that they have a duty to inform the clergy of the parish of the names and addresses of the seriously ill without waiting for the last moment. You should also interest members of parish groups to find this an occasion for authentic testimony of fraternal charity.

Keep a personal notebook containing a list of your sick and infirm, and the dates of the visits you have made. But it is a good thing to have a registry of the sick at the rectory.

This conforms to the directives of the ritual: "*Ad hoc iuvabit praesertim in amplis parochiis, aegrotorum notam seu catalogum habere, ut cuiusque statum et conditionem cognoscat, eorumque memoriam facilius retinere, et illis oportune subvenire possit*" (*Rituale* IV:2).

In this register, is is important to indicate which priest visited the patient, which sacraments he received, and even to give some brief indication of those present. This register will be of great help in avoiding too many visits, one priest unaware of the other's, to the same patient, or in knowing what sacraments he has received, or in planning a day of vistis to the sick.

Do not let a day pass without asking the divine Master for the gift of understanding the sick, for the power to touch their hearts and to comfort them effectively. You should also go to him to ask that none of your sick die without being reconciled to him. Sometimes you will have no exterior sign of conversion, but such a prayer cannot leave Jesus' heart untouched. You will obtain a real charism for the sick, and you will perceive that this ministry, sometimes trying and crucifying, let us admit it, is one of the most sanctifying for the soul of the priest.

When the case is an emergency, do not hesitate to leave all and go to see the person. . . .

Too often, the visit of the priest is considered the sign of near death. You can see how important it is to destroy this image. Therefore, you must avoid limiting your visits to those on the point of death. When people see that our visits do not bring death, but on the contrary calm a patient and, in some cases, contribute to the restoration of his health, they will be less afraid to call us.

It is rare that you be immediately shown the door. This will happen, however. Let it be the occasion for a time of prayer and penance. A priest should never be discouraged. It may be the occasion for enlightening the hostile family by a letter such as this, for example: "I understand how you did not receive me immediately. Undoubtedly, I came at an inconvenient time . . ." or: "Even if you would not receive me because you do not like priests, believe me, that is not what I want of you. We are at the service of all, whether they like us or not. I am certain that if you understood us, you would realize our only purpose: to console, to comfort, to do good. I would be pleased to hear news of the patient, and, if you so desire, I would like to visit him, as I visit all the sick of the neighborhood."

Most of the time, they will receive you, but with a little difficulty and hesitation. They are afraid that you will frighten the patient, so it is important that you make a good impression on your first visit. If the patient has found you amiable, those around him will welcome your return.

When you go to visit a patient, do not go with an air of condolence, nor of catastrophe, but neither indeed with an air of joviality that gives the impression you do not sympathize with his condition. Let him sense in you, above all, much kindness and a spirit of service. To sum it up, among your sick, strive to be like Jesus in your place. To do this, communicate often in his sentiments regarding them. Stay closely united to him.

Little by little, you will acquire a psychological sense of the sick. The psychology of one with pulmonary tuberculosis is different from that of one with a broken bone; that of one in a hospital from that of one in his own room; that of one injured from that of one with a fever.

Do not sit on the patient's bed, and even avoid leaning on the foot of the bed. Often the jostlings you unconsciously give the bed are disagreeable to the patient, especially a cardiac patient.

When you visit a sick person, it is necessary to talk to him and, if it is not tiring for him, it is well for him to talk. Naturally, you speak of the illness, the treatment and what the doctor has said, but we must try to get to know the patient himself. The ideal is to ask him about his work, to be interested in the techniques of his trade, to ask him for explanations. The patient will reveal himself in revealing his profession and will open the way to confidence.

Do not begin by complimenting the patient on his appearance. Immediate compliments are always suspect. He can immediately answer that it is not his appearance that is sick . . .

Do not have a systematic optimism, wishing to prove to the patient at all cost that he will be all right or will soon get better. By wishing to prove too much, you risk losing his confidence.

Make him talk about himself. Listen with patience and kindness to his complaints and his confidences. But do not seek to have him enter into too much detail.

Indeed, be interested in his illness, but do not play the

doctor. To each his own vocation; be content to stay on your own ground, that of the spirit and of charity.

Avoid as much as possible the word "resignation." It is misunderstood and can determine an inferiority complex. Confidence and filial abandon to the will of God are certainly preferable.

Remember that health is a gift of God. It must be asked for, as with all his gifts. This asking is part of the meaning of life and of the divine will. Normally, you should encourage the patient to desire a cure: acts of indifference on this subject are nothing less than acts of omission.

You have a perfect right, and often the duty, to be interested in the living conditions of the patient. But offer aid only when you are sure of being able to give it. Be careful not to lay the ground for future deceptions.

When making a visit, guard against any untimely zeal. Often, the incurable have learned to live with their misery. If you recommend that they avoid all movement, all action, you humiliate or discourage them.

Except in critical cases, give the patient an occasion to render service to others; first of all with regard to those around him by avoiding useless needs (certain patients become tyrants); then with regard to others as well.

What better way to give the patient the will to live than to lead him to an awareness that he is not totally isolated.

Never let yourself be impressed by what those about may have to say regarding the patient. Receive with deference the suggestions made to you: "Especially, Father, do not frighten him . . . Do not speak to him about confession . . ." Be tactful, but preserve your independence with regard to the soul in your charge.

Except in the case where the patient himself has asked to see a priest, or indeed is in danger of death, rarely can you give the sacraments on the first visit, or even speak of it.

There is little you can do in the case of apoplexy, an accident, or a pulmonary in the last stages; the patient is stunned by the affliction and partly unconscious. All you can attempt is an exhortation, somewhat in these terms: "I am a priest who has come to see you. . . . You recognize me, don't you? . . . You are suffering very much. . . . We will ask the good Lord to help you: 'My God, I love you; my God, pardon my sins.'"

Then: "I am going to give you the sacrament of the sick. Would you like to say the Our Father with me?" Frequently this, or the equivalent, represents the maximum effort the patient can make.

Aside from cardiacs, typhoids or those sick with a liver attack, you can try harder. Try to obtain at least the essentials of a confession: "Do you want to ask God's healing? It is possible only if you set yourself straight with him. You have not made your Easter duty for a long time, right? And you have missed Sunday Mass frequently? And then you have lied sometimes . . . Now do you want to ask pardon of God for all your sins? Say with me: 'My God, I ask your pardon. My God, I love you.' For your penance, say with me: 'Jesus, Mary, Joseph, I trust in you. My God, I accept whatever is your will.'" (This last formula is to assure the validity of the plenary indulgence "*in articulo mortis.*")

In each case, act according to the state of the penitent,

trying with much tact and kindness to obtain what is "reasonably possible."

Outside of urgent cases, you must prepare the patient to receive the sacraments. Speak of prayer in as simple a way as possible: "You have tried many remedies, but they cannot do all. Let the doctor do what he can, but he is not the Good Lord. . . . Have you asked God himself to cure you? Would you like to try to pray a little with me?" Begin with the authority of the Our Father, and it is a rare patient who will not respond. Then go on to speak of some other subject, and return to the necessity of prayer only when you are about to leave. This will leave the patient to think a little about it on his own.

When you are dealing with those not yet very far away from religious practices, you can suggest to them a novena: a novena to our Lady of Lourdes, or to St. Joseph, or to St. Theresa of the Child Jesus. At the end of such a novena, holy communion appears most fitting, and confession in preparation for receiving the Eucharist might well be in order.

But, in many cases, this would be asking too much at one time. So limit yourself to a few words on prayer. Then, one day, if you give him the opportunity, the patient will open up to you: "I have prayed, but things are not going well. . . . You can see that it has been of no avail." This is the opportune moment. In all kindness, without getting angry, you explain: "Indeed, you have prayed and it did not cure you, it is true . . . But, after all, it is partly your fault. . . . If you want God to listen to you, you must first set yourself right with him. You are well aware that you have not done this. Look, how long has it been since you made your Easter duty?" To this question thus introduced, the penitent responds easily enough, so much so that he might feel a good deal of shame for having neglected his religious practices for so long. Then continue, not in an interrogative way, but affirmatively: "During that time you missed Sunday Mass and neglected your prayers. . . ." And the confession thus initiated will generally follow to its completion without resistance.

Keep informed about the new relaxations the Church has given to the sick with regard to the sacraments, especially concerning the dispensation from the eucharistic fast.

When you have administered the sacraments to the sick person, do not then leave him. Often, on the contrary, from this moment you can help him produce truly supernatural acts of offering his sufferings and accepting death, if death is imminent. Until he has made his confession, the patient senses deeply what you want of him, and this creates something of a trial for him. Once the difficult step is taken, there is no ulterior motive, and one speaks indeed as a friend. This is the moment of confidences and often the occasion to fill out what could be but a summary in the first confession.

It must be said, in our hurried ministry, that there is a real temptation to neglect those in the extremity of their sickness. At the end of a tiring day, one should indeed find the means to go see an ailing person whose soul inspires disquieting thoughts, and this is all the more difficult if the patient has been "made ready." Yet, it is of capital importance for the patient and those about him. It is active proof that you are visiting the sick not just "for the sacraments," but because you are really interested.

Choose the time of your ordinary visits to the sick. Avoid the morning, the time for housekeeping.

In general, do not go beyond twenty minutes, and make it even briefer if the patient is feverish.

Do not have a hurried air, no matter how brief the visit. Give yourself entirely to the patient.

Taking leave of a sick person is an art you will learn little by little. Sometimes you can say a prayer with him. At other times, you will give him your blessing. But, in general, do not leave in silence. Stand up in the middle of a sentence, and finish it while standing. Then you part with wishes for prompt recovery and your promise to return soon.

Avoid conversations in the hallway with the family. The patient is jealous of his independence and his intimacy. Some are very susceptible and fear a lack of discretion in the priest.

The sick get the habit of having a priest visit them; they count on it and, on occasion, when other work has carried him beyond the usual date, they reproach him for forgetting them. As a mean, a visit every two weeks seems to suffice for those with long-term maladies such as tuberculosis or cancer; a weekly visit for short-term maladies. With those suffering from gravely advanced illnesses, if they are well disposed toward receiving the priest, we may be obliged to make a visit every two days or even every day, but a very short one. With a little experience, you will be able easily enough to see whether the patient is content with the visit he receives or if it is a burden to him. It remains only to regulate the length and frequency of your visits in consequence.

You render a great service to those suffering long-term maladies when you encourage them to enter Catholic organizations for the sick (Apostolate of Suffering, Catholic Union of the Sick in America, League of Shut-In Sodalists),[1] and if you make them beneficiaries of works done in their service (libraries for the sick, pilgrimages to Lourdes, our Lady of Perpetual Help, etc.).

Youths who are sick can be directed to the different branches of the Extension Society, or to different specialized movements: Scouts, CYO, Sodalities of our Lady, etc.

By visiting the sick regularly, you will gain important experience of human misery and suffering in all its forms. In more than one case you will find examples of courage, generosity and love of the cross. You will also gain an admirable understanding of your parish.

As to the patient, you can do good to both his entire family and to his neighbors. You will be the subject of family conversations, and on your attitude will depend a reign of sympathy or, on the contrary, of antipathy toward the Church.

Finally, some of the sick can, through their communion in the passion of Christ, become precious auxiliaries for your apostolate.

[1] See Appendix.

8   THE YOUNG PRIEST AND CATECHETICS

Religious instruction is generally the first ministry to which the young priest is called. This is surely one of the most rewarding and most necessary ministries.

What could be more rewarding than to reveal to the souls of children and prospective converts the infinite beauty, majesty and love of Christ who lives in them and they in him?

What could be more necessary right now, when the only religious knowledge so many children have is what we give them?

Catechesis is one of the first means the young priest should employ to fulfill his mission to teach: *Euntes docete.*

But this teaching should not be like that of a professor conducting his course, but more like that of an apostle who puts his heart into it and forms as well as informs the children.

The purpose of catechetics is not to prepare children only for their first communion—which, in that case, might be their last. It is not just to put into their heads abstract ideas which, as someone once observed, "will not stay with them a hundred yards down the street." It is supposed to be an apprenticeship in the truths of the Christian life.

In this regard, one of the pioneers in the catechetical renewal, Josef A. Jungmann, has remarked:

Catechesis and preaching are the two chief ways in which the Church exercises her teaching office. Whereas the sermon is limited to certain definite occasions, takes up and evaluates certain definite points of doctrine, and through them seeks to keep alive and to develop Christian life, catechesis furnishes a basic introduction to the whole of Christian doctrine. Today in most Christian countries catechesis is concerned with the younger generation who, as infants, were adopted into the kingdom of grace by baptism. After their mental faculties have awakened and before the children go into the wider life of the world, it attempts to familiarize them with the doctrines of their faith and to show them the way of salvation. From this it is evident that catechesis is one of the most rewarding tasks of pastoral work . . .[1]

Let us, therefore, be aware of our responsibilities. This is undoubtedly the only normal contact most of the children will have with the supernatural and perhaps even with the priest.

It is all the more important to take special care in this religious formation, since the child is at that unique age of privileged periods which Maria Montessori calls the *sensitive periods*. What is not assimilated at this period can never be assimilated in the same manner with as much facility.

The child of seven to twelve years is also at the age when he is in a position to make much moral progress and when it is possible to determine many of the dominant traits in his character which puberty will fix almost definitively.

[1] *Handing on the Faith*, New York 1962, xi.

A priest should never forget the commandment Christ addressed to all: "And you shall be witnesses for me." Our ambition should be to make all our children Christians who will bear witness to Christ by their entire life, ready, if need be, to testify by their blood. Those who observe their lives should find these witnesses of Christ living motives for faith.

"Nothing is likely to turn souls from God more than religious doctrine which has become a discourse instead of a way of life" (Maurice Zundel).

It is not just a question of teaching truths, but of awakening faith by uniting each creature to him who is the Truth, and of making his influence spread through all of life.

The child's first contact with the priest is of capital importance. Thus the importance of a greeting, of a smile, of kindness. Should it not be through the priest first of all that the child discovers God? Each of our little ones should, in his turn, be able to answer in the words of that child of Ars: "How good God must be, for Father is so good!"

The child will go with confidence to someone he knows loves him. It is never a waste of the catechist's time to collect his thoughts for a few minutes before the class and to fill his heart with Christ's love for each of these souls whom he has a mission to conduct to him.

The children must sense that we are in contact with God in the intimate depths of our hearts and that it is God who has made us what we are in their regard.

It is a grave error to begin by turning to the catechism and to lessons to be learned. We must first put the children in contact with God, as the first apostles did with the first

Christians. Long and lovingly did they recount the life of the divine Master that their hearers might learn to know and to love him.

Bishop Landrieux, Bishop of Dijon, expressed this idea clearly as far back as 1922, in his pastoral letter, "Teaching the Gospel for the First Time":

The catechism is always a lesson. The Gospel is a history. Why wish to teach as a lesson what we can teach as a story? The child sits through a lesson, but he never tires of stories. The child does not listen to a story as we do, as outsiders with a remote curiosity that makes us listen as foreigners to the action. The child enters into it. With his imagination and feelings, he puts himself completely within the action. He forms pictures of everything and brings it all to life. If we speak of our Lord, of his life or his actions, in simple accounts colored with parables, in their Palestinian setting, with the marvelous element of the miracles through which his divinity shines, the child will see him, listen to him, hear him and follow him. Soon he will learn to love him. And, if we take care to orient his faith, his heart and his piety toward the tabernacle so that he can recall constantly that the Jesus of the Gospel is himself, hidden there, living with us and for us in this sacrament, then the work of religious formation and education will be an easy task.

The grand gesture of St. John the Baptist should be the familiar gesture of the true catechist: "Ecce Agnus Dei," pointing your finger at the tabernacle while explaining the Gospel. . . .

It is important that their early learning be interesting for them and not fatiguing, that they find it attractive, that they find it enjoyable, that they love it. For, if the first contact with religion is trying, the first impression disagreeable, if we at first impose on them too heavy a burden, they will lose heart and carry unpleasant memories with them forever.

Explanations, no matter how complete and wise, are bound to remain sterile if there is no conviction behind them.

Only when our children have a heart taken up by our Lord can we obtain from them the effort to study his doctrine deeply.

Let us use a little ingenuity to make our classes attractive and varied. We have to prepare the class well in advance, composing songs we shall have them sing, prayers we shall have them say, advice we shall give, resolutions we shall suggest, pictures or slides we intend to explain.

We must know how to use the help of the men and women of the CCD and the help of the children themselves.

These CCD workers may be from the parish or from outside the parish. We have a right to expect regular attendance of them, and at least a minimum of doctrinal and pedagogic competence. They have the right to expect of us a worthwhile mission. They deserve to be encouraged and supported in their work with the children.

The children themselves can be utilized advantageously as group leaders or as class monitors. Some will be very proud of such a role and will be the first to benefit from it. Perhaps they will ask us to form a preparatory study circle for them, to put them ahead in their studies, and to prepare them to answer the questions their comrades might ask.

Let us go to our catechism classes confidently. We have an ally here, the Holy Spirit. Let us not forget that these children have been baptized, that they are already sons of

God the Father and living members of Christ. Already they possess, in a rudimentary state, that sense of the faith known as the "germen fidei," and, too, they possess those supernatural instincts, so powerful at their age, which are the gifts of the Holy Spirit.

Above all, our role is to dispose our children properly to the action of grace. In other words, we must aid them to say "yes" or, rather, to do "yes" to God. He awaits only this "yes" to act and increase in them.

We might say that the child is at the age where he finds himself on equal footing with the supernatural. Neither does the mysterious frighten him, nor does the marvelous surprise him. Doubt flourishes only after those about him have troubled or trampled his confidence.

True, many of our children have been raised in a pagan atmosphere where religion, too often misunderstood, is deformed and turned to ridicule. But, do not forget it, the infant himself is disposed to believe. Skepticism is against his nature. It is always a heterogeneous product coming from the adult, and it remains superficial to his soul until puberty. Contact with a priest of radiant faith and burning charity can suffice to melt it away forever and transform the child into a leader in his milieu.

Never think that because you are dealing with children you can alter without blame the truths of our faith. However, you are using truths which our scholastic formation leads us to present in a purely notional and consequently too abstract manner, so you must translate them into language the child's intelligence can assimilate. An Italian proverb affirms that every translator more or less betrays the thought of the author: "*Traduttore traditore.*" A deep knowledge of theology is necessary to be sure of not betraying the truth in trying to translate it.

In their own interest, our kindness to the children should coincide with a certain firmness as to order and discipline. The child, who understands admirably how to create disorder, loves above all what is well ordered. The priest who, while always kind, knows how to make himself obeyed and respected, will have more influence and will be more loved in the end than one who lets everything go.

Without discipline, the classes become more difficult for everyone, especially the catechist, and unprofitable for the children. Discipline is, above all, a question of climate. The ideal is that discipline never be questioned. When it is understood from the first that in religion class conduct is better than anywhere else, that nobody speaks without permission to speak, that nobody turns his head, but looks straight ahead, that eyes are always on the priest, then the tone is set and anything else will seem strange even to the children.

If, on the other hand, the session is lively, interesting, and varied, if moments of relaxation (singing, group responses, practical projects, outside lessons) judiciously follow periods of sustained attention, the children will be caught up in the action and, without too much effort, profit to the maximum.

By our own attitude, our tone of voice, we ourselves should inspire an impression of religious respect when we teach catechism.

The environments in which our children live have

lost the sense of the sacred. We have to restore it, occasionally pressing it and insisting on it. "*Sancte sancta*"; holy things are to be treated in a holy way. But first, we must be deeply penetrated by this attitude.

What the child will contemplate is our contemplation. What will make the child pray is our real prayer. Before beginning to pray, stir up in them all, and in yourself first of all, a realization of the presence of God; demand correct posture; use a moderate and respectful tone of voice, a moderate speed. Let us be enemies of speed, of garbling, of raised voices. And, above all, let us not be content to preside or direct; let us, too, pray interiorly.

One of the primary duties of the catechist is to awaken in the child the sense and the taste for prayer. To do this, let it spring spontaneously from the lesson or from what is going on at the time. Suggest simple and short formulas which the children will repeat after you to themselves or out loud. Better yet, let the children propose them, and you will sometimes be surprised by what they are capable of discovering by themselves.

Pope Pius XI's encyclical on education demands the *active and gradually ever more conscious cooperation of the child in his own formation.* Is it not in the matter of spiritual and moral education that there is the greatest need to appeal to what is best in the soul of the baptized?

Nothing is more contrary to the spirit of the Church and to good child psychology than keeping them passive and immobile. "Inertia in a child," says Dr. Lauffer, the French psychiatrist, "is pathological, and prolonged immobility is prejudicial to his power of acquisition."

There is considerable advantage in holding these meetings someplace other than the church. There, you run the risk of frequent disorder; the children are often distracted by people coming and going. Your appeals for order will distract from the majesty of the holy place. Finally, your children, obliged to speak out loud, are in danger of losing some of the respect and spirit of contemplation the house of God demands.

Then, too, the house of God does not lend itself very well to the execution of practical projects, group meetings, the showing of slides, and so forth.

If you have a building at your disposal, arrange it so the children can have the pleasure of coming there, of exploring it. Make it proper, uncluttered, decorated in as great a part as possible by the students themselves. Not too many statues, but use drawings, maxims, posters and pictures. Renew them from time to time.

Make it practical with solid tables and chairs, but mobile enough for group activities, recitation circles and easy arrangement along the walls for a stage play. Blackboards, geographical maps, wall pictures, slide projectors, etc. are useful equipment.

There is, of course, the greatest of merit in not having the young and the old in the same class. You cannot speak to both in the same language; the teaching method and the projects cannot be the same.

The regularity of catechism classes must be preserved at all cost. If you are kept from it for some grave reason, sickness or urgent sick calls, for example, it is better to have a lay teacher take the class rather than call it off.

It is important that the scheduled meeetings be held on a fixed day and at a fixed hour. Indeed, inasmuch as possible, always the same day and the same hour lest the children, routine by nature, become easily disorganized.

May you never be obliged to change the time of catechism to be present at a burial or marriage. "Catechism is sacred!"

Whenever you conduct your classes on the very person of our Lord for the little ones, concentrate on his life and his miracles.

The difficulty with many manuals is that they are presented as the uniform development of equal chapters without emphasizing the essential ideas.

But the book is only a tool; the value of the work depends above all on the worker.

Make your own brief synthesis of the principal themes of the catechism. In preparing your catechism lesson:

1. See which central idea the chapter is related to.

2. Find all the comparisons, stories (especially from salvation history and the Gospel), pictures, prayers and songs that will help the children to understand and assimilate the matter.

3. Sum up the essentials of the lesson in a few short sentences. If possible, make them rhythmic.

4. Have the children write them out, say them aloud. Let them become something like slogans or maxims which they should be able to recall all their lives.

5. Foresee, or let the children discover for themselves, practical applications (activities, resolutions, efforts) which should have immediate effects in the children's lives and

rise from what they have just learned from the catechism.

Do not forget that a truth is not fully learned until it is "acted upon." A child is not to go to Christ with his heart and mind only, but also with his lips and eyes and ears.

Always check to see whether or not the child has understood completely, or whether he has taken the accessory for the essential. Be careful of the words you employ; the vocabulary of the child, even in the city, is extremely restricted. Parroting, he is perfectly capable of repeating words (at the risk of mispronouncing them) without knowing their meaning, or giving them a meaning altogether different from what they really are.

Be careful too of comparisons. Not that you should not use them; they are an excellent pedagogic device. But every comparison limps (comparison is not reason). If you are not on your guard, there is indeed a danger that the child, who by nature thinks simply, will be aware only of the image that illustrates an aspect of the truth, but will not see the relation of the metaphor to the idea. This will result in such disconcerting definitions as: *the Trinity is a triangle; grace is an electric lamp.*

Quiz the children often. Let them explain the truths they have learned not in formulas they have memorized, but in their own words—as if they had to explain them to an unbelieving friend.

Recall the educational precepts of the elderly Montaigne. They are even more valid for religion than for any other field of knowledge.

To learn by heart is not to learn; it is to guard in your memory what has been given to you. What one really learns, he makes use of without looking to a teacher, without turning his eyes to his book. What false sufficiency is a purely bookish sufficiency.

Let the educator demand of the child not just an account of the words of the lesson, but their sense and substance. And let the child judge the good he has done not by the testimony of his memory, but by the testimony of his life.

Whatever the subject being learned, the teacher will have him portray it under a hundred aspects, and relate it to as many different subjects, to see if he has yet understood it well and made it his own.

To keep their attention, first pose your question, then designate the child who is to answer. To avoid all disorder, let it be known that nobody is to answer unless he is asked.

For those eleven years and older, you can assign written compositions from time to time.

Use the board and slides generously. Visual memory is the best developed with children. But take care—the child does not have the synthetic spirit. He notices the details but does not pick out the general idea. At seven, he sees objects without on his own seeing the connection they relate; for example: a man, a boy, a car. From nine to twelve years, he begins to discover the relation: "This is a man pushing a car with a boy." Only after twelve years is he able to interpret: "A man is out of gas and the son is helping the father to push the car." So, do not fail to interpret the pictures you show them, or else have them interpreted under your control.

Let your children play. Do not object. The old philosopher Ribot wrote: "The child develops his attention, and so his faculties of acquisition, better by active and lively play than by passive and abstract study." Even before him, in 1856, Father Icard, superior general of Saint-Sulpice, said the same thing calling, if you please, on the authority of the councils: ". . . the councils ordain that we make catechetical instruction so easy and agreeable that it be presented to the children under the appearance of an interesting and agreeable game, rather than under that of a serious and difficult study."

Some years ago, in a conference to the Catholic Institute of Paris on the history of the psychology of language, Father Jousse affirmed that it is of the child's very nature to reproduce with his whole body a veritable *mimodrame* of whatever has struck his heart or his imagination. For him, this is the best way to assimilate an idea or reinforce a feeling.

Fénelon thought the same thing. Thus he recommended that children be accustomed to represent the persons of salvation history to themselves:

Let them take such and such a parable, such and such a scene from the Gospel, or simply some aspect of life the lesson deals with, and let them reproduce it in a living picture, unanimated or animated, with or without words. Give them only the idea, and let them search for themselves, Gospel in hand. You will be surprised at the interest they will take, whether as spectators or as actors. But you will be surprised, too, at the sincerity, the freshness of expression, and the emotion that will develop in them all. Then it will be easy for you to make prayer and practical application flow spontaneously.

Let these game sessions be taken seriously, for "the child does not play in order to laugh." Let it take place among themselves, without outside spectators, and let them preserve an eminently formative religious character.

You can propose other activities to the children, with the liberty of doing them individually or in teams: drawing, map drawing, posters cut from paper, molding, pottery, models—which will be as much modes of expression as aids to memory.

It is all the harder to forget that on which one has labored intently for many hours.

Do not fail to have your children sing. But choose your hymns; *to sing a hymn is to pray twice* is an old tradition of Saint-Sulpice. Yes, but on condition you sing well. Choose hymns whose words are suitable for the children and which do not express exaggerated sentiments in mordant terms (for example: *tears of blood, tongue of fire*, etc.).

It is hard for the child to pay attention to two things at once. He will follow the melody without paying attention to the text. So it is well to have him read each verse out loud and to explain it to him before singing it.

"We will have done a poor job of making the catechism a center of Christian formation if, parallel the effort we make regarding the child, we make no effort to influence the family, for it is the family that will finally have the last word" (Canon Boyer).

It is very important to understand the family atmosphere in which the child has been brought up. Beyond the child, always see his parents. These years of catechism can be years of grace for them. Canon Boyer continues:

This contact can be assured by visits to the families, for example, when a child is sick, or when a child has been absent (we should never go to see the family to complain about a child; in such a case, it is better to invite the family to come to see us).

This contact can be kept up too by a monthly correspondence card indicating grades for conduct, application, lessons, projects, and composition—with a few lines in your own hand. This card should be signed by the parents. They are generally attentive about reading notes from teachers about their children.

In some parishes, all of the parents come to the teacher only on the vigil of first communion for some practical directives. This is indeed insufficient.

There should be a meeting with all the parents at least every three months in the form of a catechetical day, a day of exposition, or simply a day of pedagogical discussion. The greatest interest on this day will be to explain to them what goes on at catechism and how they can fulfill their part in the religious education of their children.

Parents are generally appreciative of what is done for their children. The parents are in great part responsible for the perseverance of the students. Most of the time, when children do not continue, it is the fault of their family. If parents were convinced of the importance of the serious Christian life, and if, on the other hand, they were made more aware of their responsibility and mission as educators, the perseverance of their children would be assured.

What we have taught our children between eight and eleven years old is hardly enough religious instruction for their entire life. Take special care to teach the lesson of perseverance. Among the ideas you have incessantly repeated during the years of religious instruction preparatory to the ceremony called first communion, it is necessary to return ceaselessly to the idea of perseverance and the missionary responsibility.

On arriving at catechism, the children of Bon-Conseil at Paris saw this sentence written on the blackboard: "It is useless to make our first communion," and Father Esquerré made it sound throughout the world, ". . . if we are not determined to persevere." Then he added: "A Christian is an apostle; if not, he is an apostate. You must be Christ's missionaries. How will you defend and spread your religion if you know it but poorly?"

After the reception of confirmation, it is time to put your catechism of perseverance to work. Make it a solemn occasion and one in which they are proud to take part.

Give to this new stage of religious education a different allure from that of previous years. Bolster your program over two years by giving a more doctrinal, historical and social course. Multiply the teamwork; switch at times to study groups. But continue to sum up in brief formulas which will remain in the hearts of your youths as forceful ideas to live by.

The study of religion will be sterile if it is not adapted to the problems of life the child will meet once he leaves us and is again in his family, school and neighborhood. This is why catechism should be concerned with the entire life of the child and should be completed by joining a group which will make his apprenticeship in the Christian life operative in the totality of daily reality.[1]

[1] See Appendix.

9 THE YOUNG PRIEST AND PRIESTLY VOCATIONS

Every priest should be concerned about priestly vocations, but the young priest seems to be given a special grace to attract young souls to the service of the Lord.

The freshness of his priesthood, the enthusiasm of his youth, the gift he has to win the heart of those youths who benefit from his early ministry, all contribute to help him awaken vocations.

Take note of your responsibilities. Tell yourself that it would be unpardonable of you not to place this concern in the first rank of your prayer intentions and in your apostolic preoccupations.

The question of vocations is all the more urgent in that the crisis in priestly recruitment is grave and because present disorders, caused by two successive wars, only aggravate it.

The first duty that falls upon you, faithful to *rogate ergo Dominum messis*, is, then, not to let a day pass without asking of God the gift of awakening numerous and holy priestly vocations. This is a prayer that rarely goes unanswered.

Create around yourself an atmosphere favorable to the blossoming of vocations. Ask the holy souls you meet to

pray for this intention, the sick you visit, the children themselves. One day or another, one of them will ask the question: "Why not me?"

In religion classes, do not be afraid to speak often of the
priesthood, of the beauty of the priestly life, and even of
the importance of his role even from the purely social point
of view. Point out the urgent need of souls and of parishes;
explain how and why one becomes a priest. Recount a few
good histories of vocations, some lives of holy priests, such
as St. Vincent de Paul, the Curé of Ars, St. John Bosco, or
lives yet nearer to us, such as Father Dismas Clark, John
XXIII, Father Alfred Delp, St. Pius X, or others.

To make the ground where the grace of a vocation may
germinate more favorable, develop among your children:

1. The *sense of the sacred*, that is, respect for God and
for sacred things.

2. The *spirit of sacrifice*—is not the priesthood the im-
molation of the soul joined to that of Christ? Perhaps the
dwindling number of persevering vocations can be attrib-
uted to the dwindling spirit of sacrifice in many families,
even Christian families.

3. The *ardent zeal for souls*—is this not the meaning of
the *misereor super turbam* which is the touchstone of the
better vocations?

Without a doubt, the priestly vocation is from God:
nemo vocatus nisi a Deo. But God calls far more children
than anyone believes. St. John Bosco did not hesitate to say
that a third of Christian sons are called, but that nine-
tenths of the chosen do not answer the call through the

fault of the children themselves (liberty is not an empty word), through the fault of the family (how many strive to snuff out vocations at their first spark), and through the fault of those priests who did not know how to express the divine appeal at the opportune moment.

In the matter of vocations, one must be bold and prudent at the same time.

Bold, because the case is relatively rare where a boy will come to you spontaneously to confide to you his desire to become a priest. So it is necessary, without of course exerting any pressure, to propose to this or that child the idea of the priesthood.

Prudent, for it is necessary to act with sure knowledge.

This classic rule will help you to recognize those boys who might have a vocation to the priesthood: health, intelligence, prudence and holiness.

Health: there is a minimum of physical health necessary to fulfil the obligations of the priesthood.

Intelligence: a minimum of intellectual ability is also necessary to carry out the required studies.

Prudence: this is not the wisdom of the child who is gentle and obedient. Rather it is that good sense, that judgment, that mental equilibrium which is so necessary for a director of souls.

Holiness: this is evidently not a consummate sanctity, nor a demand for perfection beyond the child's age. It is that holiness proportionate with the child's soul, made up of personal piety, right conscience, loyal generosity and true charity.

Cardinal Verdier, when he was the superior of the Carmelite seminary, summed up his criteria in these two questions:

1. *Does this child show signs of being able to be happy in the priesthood?*

2. *Does he have what it takes to do the job well?*

When, having presented the idea of the priesthood to a child, he refuses, do not insist and, this goes without saying, do not be harsh with him. God wants only volunteers; recall the story of the rich young man. Besides, your question will not be completely without effect. Perhaps the idea will make its own way and, one day, he will be led to a faithful study of the question on his own to find out whether he is or is not truly called to our Lord's service in the priestly life.

Whatever happens, you will have done your duty.

If the boy spontaneously speaks to you about becoming a priest, or even if your word permits him to recognize the divine call, do not rush; do not make a hasty decision. For example, if the young candidate has revealed his desire to you at summer camp in August, do not send him to enter the minor seminary in September.

Give it some time. Let this yet frail seed develop for a few months, perhaps a year, under your watchful eye.

In the course of these months, verify the purity of his intention (it is not impossible to find children who accept the idea of entering the seminary to look good in the eyes of their pastor, or to please a pious parent who desires it more than they do).

Verify also his suitability, taking into account his psychological make-up and the possibilities of his age, and direct the seriousness and sincerity of his efforts.

If your young aspirant is a student in a Catholic high school and can pursue his secondary studies under these same conditions, do not take him out. His vocation can fortify itself there without the danger of disorientation should he change his mind.

Even if he is a day student in a public school, if he can take part in a Catholic group (CYO, etc.), it is most often in his interest to let him remain there. Thanks to the many occasions that will be offered him for the apostolate and to affirm his faith, his vocation can only season. His piety, too, will become somewhat more spontaneous, somewhat more apostolic as a result. And there also, if he has a "change of mind," your young man will not suffer loss therefrom.

In these two cases, you have both the advantage of being able to be in contact with him and to keep him in contact with the life and work of the parish.

There is also the solution of day school seminaries in dioceses which have them. Unfortunately, they are in a small minority.

However, most of the time you will look to entry into the minor seminary. But first comes the question of the family's consent. As often as possible, let the boy have the opportunity to speak with his parents first, even if and especially if you have some reason to fear that the response will be negative.

In this way the child begins to fight for his vocation, commits himself for it, and begins to insure that the decision to answer "present!" to the call of God comes from him.

But if at the beginning of his vocation you leave some doubt that can have grave consequences in the future, this child will have reason later on for saying: "I was not the one who decided; someone decided for me."

Once the youth has made the first step, it is easier for you, after consulting the pastor, to invite the parents in and to explain to them that it is for their child's happiness and in their own interest not to oppose automatically a call from God as a matter of course. Indeed, rare are the parents who will not accept at least a try.

In case of a categorical refusal, do not insist. If the youth perseveres "in his idea," he will end up obtaining the realization of his desire. Opposed vocations are many times the best vocations.

Once entry into the minor seminary is decided, it is for you to present the candidate to the superior. Accompanied by a priest he knows and loves, the youth will make this first contact with a new world more easily. You should also encourage him, explain to him the usages and customs of the house, and foster the true spirit in which he should obey the rule and devote himself to his work. . . .

Do not leave him once he has set foot on the seminary grounds. Without substituting yourself for his professors, continue to show him your paternal solicitude.

From time to time, if possible, go to see him or write to him. Show your interest in his studies, his grades and, especially, keep the apostolic flame burning in him. This last will be the best stimulant for his efforts and progress.

If you are led to find a benefactor to help one of your seminarians pay his tuition, see to it that the young man shows him his appreciation. However, see to it also that the aid given does not tend to some kind of property right which will naturally do harm to the liberty and legitimate independence of the future priest.

When vacation time arrives, help him to profit from it by reviving his zeal which, due to natural occupations and the emphasis given to scholastic preoccupations, may have diminished during the year of studies. Help him to win again a life of personal piety which the necessary regimentation of seminary life always places in danger of routine and formalism.

Help him to put his priestly ideal in focus year by year. Only little by little does the young seminarian acquire that concrete notion of the priesthood which will, later on, unconsciously inspire his conduct.

This notion is formed by the thousand remarks he picks up from day to day, from contact with priests he has known or even just met, and especially from the priest who has been the father of his vocation. These are the gestures, attitudes, affirmations that have struck him all the more forcefully because they were all the more closely knit into the web of his life. This is why you must gauge the repercussion of your words, why you must, even when he is older, avoid useless confidences about your little discouragements or apostolic trials.

Remind yourself that the seminarian's mentality, even the major seminarian's, is far different from that of the priest, even the young priest. By failure to realize this difference, an inconsiderate priest who would too easily relate true or imaginary deceptions runs the risk of engendering sourness or discouragement; as, on the other hand, a priest who is exalted and only a bit of a psychologist can engender false spirits or imbalance.

If it is an excellent thing to bring the seminarian to a progressive realization of the concrete conditions in which he is to carry on his priestly ministry, it is extremely dangerous as well as out of place, under the pretext of ridding him of illusions, to criticize fellow priests and, a *fortiori*, to put the seminary and his professors on trial in his presence. The young have too much of a tendency toward independence and meaningless criticism for you to be careless about preserving respect for authority among them.

Be careful, too, about certain paradoxes or quips which can surprise or even shock a youth whose judgment is not yet mature enough to make the necessary qualifications.

In other words, he will model his priestly ideal little by little on your life as a priest. Let your priestly life be such as to inspire all the seminarians who approach you with the desire to be like you.

In the course of studies, you may have some drop-outs among your seminarians. Do not let it surprise you; this is the hard and redemptive price all who are involved in vocations have to pay. But above all, do not get angry with the young man, whatever the reason for his leaving. Receive him with kindness; help him to readapt himself and to reorient himself toward an apostolic life in the world, a life that can be all the more productive in that he has had the benefit of some years of religious formation that others have not received.

Who knows but that, after a few years of experience in the world, some will return to the seminary, their vocation all the more solid and generous. . . . In any case, it is your responsibility to see that all remain excellent Christians.

If you can, help them to find a position that will let them establish a happy home where their vocation may pass on to some of their children. This happens far more often than we realize.

But be reassured. You will not have only drop-outs. Take heart! Many of those you put on the road to the altar will reach it. What joy will fill your priestly heart when you impose your hands on one of your little ones, and what consolation for you at the hour of death if you can offer the Lord a crown of your priest-sons, the result of the fervor of your priesthood.

10 The Young Priest and Youth

If your pastor entrusts the young men of the parish to you, be happy and proud. It is a special apostolate for which, moreover, you are more ready for than any other. It is not such a long time since you were one of them, and it will not be too difficult for you to understand and accept them.

But, proceed carefully! Guard against two extremes, both equally harmful to your profound influence: be neither their comrade nor their captain; be a priest. If you are too familiar with them, you will lose their respect. If you are too distant, too . . . military, they will shut themselves off from you and avoid you. Be a priest, nothing but a priest, completely a priest, and you will merit and win their confidence.

You will have one of two tasks, either to take over the direction of a group that is already formed or to create a new one.

In the first case, strive as much as possible to retain what previously existed, infusing all the Christian and missionary spirit you can into it. Above all, observe. Only after a year or so, when you have won the esteem and respectful affection of all by your devotion, kindness and tact, can you wisely effect needed changes and launch, if there is room for it, a new organization. Believe me, this will not be a wasted year. This prudence will keep you from those retreats which are so prejudicial to your prestige and to the enthusiasm of your youths who are in danger of disorganization and discouragement.

In the second case, go easily. Do not make some high-sounding declaration that you are going to launch this or that. Make a serious inquiry as to the number of youths in the parish, the environments in which they live, different religious points of view, the hours at which they most often meet, the different ways they occupy their leisure time. In particular, look for those who seem to you the most dynamic, the most representative of the different environments. Sound out their desires, but do not make any premature promises. Although with younger children you have to try to have as many as possible present right from the start, with the teenagers you can rouse the interests of a solid and fervent nucleus to whom you can impart your apostolic ambitions in advance, whatever the form of the group you have chosen.

The priest's essential role in any organization of Catholic youths, whatever its form (sports team, theatrical group, choir, study group, apostolate) is to animate a truly Christian spirit. You will be the soul of your group to the extent that you are able to create a supernatural climate impregnating all human activities, and to the extent that your role as counselor, guide, in a word, director of souls for your youths is completed.

A young man needs spiritual and moral direction. His personality is not yet completely formed. He is at the age of direction, but also at the age of indecision, of tomorrowless enthusiasm, of fads and failures. Even when he is putting on a front, he is deeply aware of his weakness, and he is happy to be able to call on a moral authority who understands, bolsters and inspires him.

Do not fear to be exacting; we win the young to the extent we are demanding of them. Appeal to the best in them. The weakness of souls often comes from an ignorance of self. Reveal to a young man the aspirations and generous possibilities within him. These must be committed to good.

Since their judgment is not yet formed, and since they are at the age when it is easy to follow others, form their judgment in the light of the Gospel. They are at the age when, though wishing to proclaim their independence of their parents and teachers, they have an exaggerated tendency to social conformity. They have a special fear of opposing their milieu and of being singled out, and they willingly repeat and endorse ready-made judgments which are not their own. It is your job to safeguard their Christian personality and to help them to become the leaders who will set the tone for others through their solid personal convictions.

Give them the desire to become leaders, with all that this implies of responsibilities, necessary self-mastery and self-sacrifice for the mission of commanding and leading. This is perhaps one of the best ways of bringing them to acquire self-mastery, to love the effort that lifts, to acquire the taste for the hard things thanks to which one becomes a man.

Do not be afraid to give them ambitions, though guarding against puerile vanity. In reality, the best way to form true humility is for the youth to desire to use the talents he has received to the maximum in the service of Christ and his brothers. The Christian humility which makes him say: "Without the Lord, I can do nothing," is the stepping stone of the Christian boldness which made St. Paul say: "I can do all things in him who strengthens me."

You have a special duty to guide them in that essential education called the education of the heart and emotions. You have to aid them in the conquest of a strong and radiant purity, in the proper appraisal of the new forces they feel in themselves, and in learning to control their emotional powers for their vigorous development.

You should, of course, keep a prudent reserve with children, but with young men and women you have the right and the duty to speak clearly on such subjects as dating, love, eventual marriage, sex. Do not hesitate even to take the initiative, for often they are shy to express their problems. They are the victims of so many prejudices and so much ignorance! Where, if not from you, can they find solid moral doctrine and the meaning of the beauty and requirements of Christian love and the use of sex?

It is very important that our youths have a clear and lucid understanding of the things of love, just as God willed in the splendor of his eternal plan.

To keep their hearts pure, to impose upon themselves the real acts of vigilance human love requires, they must have a totally clear and beautiful outlook on the divine plan. They must understand that real love is something great and very beautiful and that it demands a number of conditions and sacrifices. They must understand that only this love is worth living, that it alone authorizes and justifies outward sensible signs of affection, and that to make love ahead of time, before they are married, is to compromise one's happiness and human dignity.

The spiritual and moral direction you owe your youths should seek to teach them to direct themselves in the light of Christian principles. It is not so much a question of guarding the youths about you, but of preparing them to live a truly Christian life far from you and your protection, eyes and guidance.

Never present Christianity simply as a code of prohibitions, but as a richness that transfigures their human life and gives the true meaning of problems that can arise: work, love, family, society, friendship, etc.

In the organization of your youth groups, be careful not to do everything yourself. Be careful not to make yourself irreplaceable. Do not agree to launch a new organization unless you have the supports to sustain it. The ministry of youth is a most engaging ministry in every sense of the word, that is, passionate but also very absorbing. Give yourself whole-heartedly, but do not let yourself be captured by it.

Keep some time for yourself to reflect, to work, to pray. If you do not, at the end of a few years you will have nothing more to give.

Be careful of periods of "flashes of inspiration": fairs, rummage sales, theatrical productions. If you have not learned to distribute the work to responsible and capable people, you will run the risk of being overburdened both physically and morally.

What should we think of sports? Many youths will ask for them. In fact, moderate use of sports can be excellent. It is not only a salutary diversion, but an exercise which is beneficial from the moral as well as physical point of view, for it can develop a team spirit and a taste for effort. There is the good-sport spirit, the fair play, which can have fortunate consequences for the lives of the young.

But there is a danger, that of excessive involvement, together with all the inconveniences caused by the continual trips competition requires.

If there are teams among your parish groups, seek to channel their activities; see their team captains frequently; work on the group through them. See to it that the sports fans give sports their proper place in the Christian conception of life, and that they preserve or rediscover the taste for the things of the soul.

If sports teams do not exist, introduce them only if you have the proper know-how and only after you are sure of having your team captains well in hand.

If you have many Catholic groups in your parish, corresponding to the various interests and needs of your youths, see to it that you are the father of all and not just the chaplain for one class or clan. Be equally the father of those who do not come into the area of your work. Do not forget that you share in your pastor's missionary responsibility for all the young souls of your parish.

Among all your youths, whatever group they belong to, strive to create a parish-family spirit. Without interfering with the respective programs of the different movements, facilitate fraternal encounters and fields of common action. Organize a real parish house for the young where they can feel at home among themselves, where they can find— thanks to the priest who is their father—what Monsignor Fillon called "the community of worship, of piety and of Christian relaxation." It is true that there are youths who, rightly or wrongly, cannot or will not let themselves get involved in a group. There are others who, in a moment of crisis, will abandon a particular activity. But it is well for youths to have this place of welcome where they can remain in contact with your priestly soul, and, through you, with the parish family of youths.

Little by little, according to the helps you have been able to arrange, you can organize a certain number of common services for the use of all: a library, hikes, dances, picnics.

You can, as well, without prejudicing the special days of recollection of each group, organize monthly parish retreats.

Perhaps you could also organize an association of Marian devotion or a Franciscan or Dominican Third Order for the more fervent members of each group. More souls than we realize are capable of a very intense spiritual life and need only a stimulant and the grace of a pious group to tend toward a truly ideal sanctity. When this pious group develops among its members the life of prayer, the spirit of sacrifice and apostolic charity, be assured by that very fact of the recruitment of the most solid and most devoted of your faithful Catholics.

Hold periodic meetings with your different group leaders, that is, with all to whom you have entrusted some responsibility. This especially is your opportunity to set the tone, to create a spirit of unity while, at the same time, keeping the missionary flame burning in all. This is also your opportunity to form the souls of your Christian leaders who will multiply your action and allow your work to continue after you by giving it a truly institutional character.

Here we offer to our young coworkers in the priesthood some addresses which we hope they will find useful either for themselves or for their ministry. Clearly these lists, giving only the official titles and addresses of organizations and publications, do not claim to be exhaustive. Naturally the addresses given are subject to change.

1. Priestly Associations

American Catholic Correctional Chaplains, P.O. Box 455, Ramsey, Ill. 62080.

Catholic Homiletic Society, Techny, Ill. 60082.

Chaplains' Aid Association, Inc., 29 E. 50 Street, New York, N.Y. 10022.

National Clergy Conference on Alcoholism, P.O. Box 1194, Indianapolis, Ind. 46206.

Priests' Eucharistic League, 194 E. 76 Street, New York, N.Y. 10021.

2. Periodicals of Interest to Priests

Catechetical:

Good Tidings, 11 Park Place, New York, N.Y. 10072.

The Living Light, National Center of Confraternity of

Christian Doctrine, 1312 Massachusetts Avenue N.W., Washington, D.C. 20005.

Lumen Vitae, 184 Rue Washington, Brussels 5, Belgium.

Our Parish Confraternity, 1312 Massachusetts Avenue N.W., Washington, D.C. 20005.

The Sower, 11 Cavendish Square, London W. 1, England.

Teaching All Nations, East Asian Pastoral Institute, P.O. Box 1815, Manila, P.I.

Others:

American Ecclesiastical Review, 620 Michigan Avenue N.E., Washington, D.C. 20017.

The Bible Today, St. John's Abbey, Collegeville, Minn. 56321.

Catholic Biblical Quarterly, The Catholic Biblical Association of America, Washington, Cardinal Station, D.C. 20017.

Chicago Studies, Box 655, Mundelein, Ill. 60060.

Christ to the World, Via G. Nicotera, 31 - Rome (9), Italy.

The Clergy Review, 14 Howick Place, Westminster, London, S.W. 1, England.

The Ecumenist, Glen Rock, N.J. 07450.

Emmanuel, 194 E. 76 Street, New York, N.Y. 10021.

Guide, 411 W. 59 Street, New York, N.Y. 10019.

Herder Correspondence, 232 Madison Avenue, New York, N.Y., 10016.

The Homiletic and Pastoral Review, 53 Park Place, New York, N.Y. 10017.

Journal of Ecumenical Studies, Duquesne University, Pittsburgh, Pa. 15219.

Liturgy, 3428 Ninth Street N.E., Washington, D.C. 20017.

The Priest, Noll Plaza, Huntington, Ind. 46750.

Priestly Studies, Old Mission, Santa Barbara, Calif. 93105.

The Pope Speaks, 3622 12 Street N.E., Washington, D.C. 20017.

Scripture, 24 Golden Square, London, W. 1, England.

Social Action Notes for Priests, 1312 Massachusetts Avenue N.W., Washington, D.C. 20005.

Theology Digest, St. Mary's College, St. Marys, Kansas 66536.

Theological Studies, Woodstock, Maryland 21163.

Worship, St. John's Abbey, Collegeville, Minn. 56321.

3. ASSOCIATIONS FOR THE SICK

Apostolate of Suffering, 1551 N. 34 Street, Milwaukee, Wis. 53205.

Apostolate to Aid the Dying (Markham Prayer Card Apostolate), Franciscan Sisters of the Poor, St. Clare Convent, 60 Compton Road, Cincinnati, Ohio 45215.

Catholic Union of the Sick in America, Inc., 100 E. 50 Street, Apt. 39A, New York, N.Y. 10022.

League of Shut-In Sodalists, Marcus, Iowa 51035.

4. Some Lay Organizations

Apostleship of Prayer (League of the Sacred Heart) 515 E. Fordham Road, Bronx, N.Y. 10458.

Central Association of the Miraculous Medal, 475 E. Chelten Avenue, Philadelphia, Pa. 19144.

Christian Family Movement, 1655 W. Jackson Boulevard, Chicago, Ill. 60612.

Christopher Movement, 16 E. 48 Street, New York, N.Y. 10017.

Cursillos de Cristiandad, 909 E. Washington Street, Phoenix, Ariz. 85034.

Family Rosary, Inc., 773 Madison Avenue, Albany, N.Y. 12208.

Holy Name Society, 141 E. 65 Street, New York, N.Y. 10021.

Knights of Columbus, 78 Meadow Street, New Haven, Conn. 06707.

National Liturgical Conference, Inc., 3428 Ninth Street N.E., Washington D.C. 20017.

Paulist League, 415 W. 59 Street, New York, N.Y. 10019.

Pontifical Association of the Holy Childhood, 800 Allegheny Avenue, Pittsburgh, Pa. 15233.

Serra International, 22 W. Monroe Street, Chicago, Ill. 60603.

Society for the Propagation of the Faith, 366 Fifth Avenue, New York, N.Y. 10001.

Young Ladies' Institute, 50 Oak Street, San Francisco, Calif. 94102.

Young Men's Institute, 50 Oak Street, San Francisco, Calif. 94102.

5. Catholic Professional Organizations

American Catholic Psychological Association, Fordham University, Bronx, N.Y. 10458.

Catholic Accountants Guilds, 915 Putnam Avenue, Brooklyn, N.Y. 11221.

Catholic Library Association, 461 W. Lancaster Avenue, Haverford, Pa. 19041.

Catholic Writers' Guild of America, 65 East 89 Street, New York, N.Y. 10028.

Communication Arts Guild, 22 Friar Tuck Road, Albany, N.Y. 12203.

Druggists Guild of St. James, 918 Madison Avenue, Covington, Ky. 41011.

Guild of Catholic Lawyers, 233 Broadway Avenue, New York, N.Y. 10007.

Guild of Catholic Psychiatrists, 1703 Rhode Island Avenue, N.W., Washington, D.C. 20036.

National Association of Catholic Publishers and Dealers in Church Goods, 15 West 44 Street, New York, N.Y. 10036.

National Catholic Bandmasters' Association, Music Department, St. John's University, Collegeville, Minn. 56321.

National Catholic Pharmacists Guild of the United States, 415 County Street, New Bedford, Mass. 02740.

National Federation of Catholic Physicians' Guilds, 1438 S. Grand Boulevard, St. Louis, Mo. 63104.

6. Official National Organizations

National Center of Confraternity of Christian Doctrine, 1312 Massachusetts Avenue N.W., Washington, D.C. 20005.

National Catholic Rural Life Conference, 3801 Grand Avenue, Des Moines, Iowa 50312.

National Catholic Welfare Conference, 1312 Massachusetts Avenue N.W., Washington, D.C. 20005.

National Council of Catholic Men, 1312 Massachusetts Avenue N.W., Washington, D.C. 20005.

National Council of Catholic Women, 1312 Massachusetts Avenue N.W., Washington, D.C. 20005.